Songs from the Gallows

Galgenlieder

Translated by
Walter Arndt

Yale University Press
New Haven and London

Christian Morgenstern

Songs from the Gallows

Galgenlieder

Designed by Deborah Dutton.
Set in New Caledonia text and Syntax display types by The Composing Room of Michigan, Inc.
Printed in the United States of America by Thomson-Shore, Dexter, Michigan.

A catalogue record for this book is available from the British Library.

Library of Congress Cataloging-in-Publication Data

Morgenstern, Christian, 1871–1914.
    [Galgenlieder.   English]
    Songs from the gallows / Christian Morgenstern ; translated by Walter Arndt.
        p.   cm.
    ISBN 0-300-05278-2
    I. Title.
    PT2625.064G313   1993
    831'.912—dc20   93-3459
                                           CIP

Contents

Part Two
Palmström and Korf

**Part Three
Palma Kunkel**

Part Four
Lost in Thought

Foreword

Christian Morgenstern was born
in Munich in 1871 and died of
tuberculosis in Meran in 1914. These two years mark the
founding and the self-destruction of the second German
Empire, and—accidentally or otherwise—a refreshing
deflation of German prose and poetry from the pompous
and sentimental to the spare, sometimes otherworldly.
The literary presence of Morgenstern contributed greatly
to this clearing of the air, not by the feeble pietistic verse
he himself prized (the critics rightly called them *sinnig*
or *innig*, something like "heartfelt" or "sincere," but close
to *kitschig*), nor by his excellent translations of August
Strindberg, Knut Hamsun, and Henrik Ibsen, but by the

bizarre, incomprehensible, nonsensical, yet oddly intriguing (thus the first critics) *Songs from the Gallows,* which he published in 1905 and 1910.

Most conventional literary criteria, categories, and "fields" fail to include Morgenstern. He is neither openly didactic nor consistently satirical. If one wished to assign him to a "field," it might be shared by Lewis Carroll, overlapping with that of Wilhelm Busch's remarkable genius. He really stands alone in German literature, although some twenty years later strings similar to his were touched by Ringelnatz and even Erich Kästner.

The genre of poetry Morgenstern created belongs to the realm of the metaphysical, of subversive nonsense and superior sense. Palmström, his alter ego von Korf, his reclusive cousin Palma Kunkel, and their fleeting company of artifacts and inventions, zoological or utilitarian, are products of the same muse as Lewis Carroll's. They are emblematic figures that, as the English Germanist Leonard Forster put it, "lead their now immortal existence in realms where the burlesque has startling metaphysical implications." Morgenstern turns language inside out and discovers new shapes and inverted meanings. The procedure often undoes metaphors of millennial standing, stripping them of their conventional meanings, bringing them to a strange new life and creating new objects or activities through semantic analogies that make one's head spin; all this accompanies a rare insight into that occult interrelation between signifier and signified that has long preoccupied linguists and philosophers.

To translate Morgenstern is a rash, sometimes desperate undertaking. His verbal imagination, for all its acrobatics, is rooted in the German language, and his play with it is phonetic, semantic, and syntactic. Take *Anselm,* a harmless rustic name; change the first syllable from *an* to *un,* the negative prefix, it turns sinister, vaguely threatening; by no fault of the helpless *Selm.* Herr von Korf, so energetic, philanthropic, and inventive in his own sphere, when molested by the German bureaucracy, reminds it, and us, that he is a "congenitally disembodied naught," hence duty-free and unassailable. Animals undergo genetic metamorphoses forward or backward in time, others appear in abstract relationships with the two gentle but stubbornly elusive elves: Palmström, seemingly of Swedish parentage (if any), and von Korf, a renegade of Junker stock.

Why "gallows songs," or "songs from the gallows," or "chanties from the scaffold"? There is a parallel here to the "salons of the excluded" arranged by the unorthodox painters of Morgenstern's time in most European art centers. What animated painters, poets, and musicians was disgust with the stale, regular, literal, expected which dominated the practice of current art—also the romance of juveniles in rebellion who would not even wait to be outcast.

Morgenstern prefaces his songbook with a totally indigestible introduction—attributed to a mythical German academic—which throws the black light of lit. crit. on the movement's spirit and gestation. Here is what the butt of Morgenstern's satire, the polyparaphrastical Dr. Jeremias Müller, is made to say about the inception of the brotherhood to which he whimsically attributes some of the earliest poems:

. . . and just such a symptom, just such a symbol [of our changeful time] was the idea that on a fine day of the waning century forged together eight young men firmly resolved to confront the inimical trends of the time [I scrap here four interlocking clauses of bombast] with the burlesque show, as it were, of their humor. A strange cult united them. First, the light is strangled, then a black cloth, richly emblazoned with fearsome phosphorescent emblems, is drawn from the basket and laid on the table; at last, a single pallid taper, amid joyful-dreadful symbols drawn from the ambience of Gallows Hill. The first of the celebrants is called Owl's Hoot; he hangs highest and supplies the

sound to the breath of Crow's Carrion, who decelebrates
the Sacraments; the third is called Little Jack Ketch; he
proffers the hangman's meal; the fourth is St. Vitus
Dancer, by-named the Bellringer, for he pulls the
Death Row bell . . .

The remaining four spooks and their grisly attri-
butes are also supplied by the learned specter of the in-
troduction, with much reference forward to the songs and
irrealia in the body of the book; but the quotation above
should be enough to explain Morgenstern's title and the
atmosphere surrounding the earlier poems. What follows
below is a tenuous transposition into English of the
upstrung brotherhood's "club song":

O grue, o grue, o loathsome thing,
here by the scarlet rope we swing!
The toad has toed, the cob has spinned,
lank hanks are parted by the wind.

O grue, o grue, o fewmet foul!
You are anathem, says the owl.
It is a light, it turns to night,
but we're not there as yet, not quite,

O grue, o grue, o loathsome thing!
You hear the silver hoofbeats ring?
The scrub-owl says, "No doubt, no doubt!
Just hold your snout, just hold your snout!"

I have lived with Morgenstern and "stirred him in
my mind" (as Mary—absit sacrilegium—stirred the
angel's word in her heart) since the early thirties. It was
then that, along with a group of unorthodox classmates
and intimates, I discovered his upside-down world and
relished his peaceable insurgence against common sense,
his insouciant, liberating spirit. Although sixty years have
gone by and only a few of those particular addicts still
sing under the gallows, they undoubtedly still know much
of the corpus of 360 poems by heart, as the Anglophones

among them know the Alice books and other light verse
by heart, and for quite similar reasons.

One or the other near-bilingual member of the cal-
low Silesian disciples may have tried his hand at putting
some of Morgenstern's poems into French or, more likely,
Polish. If so, I have not seen the results. I felt strongly that
Morgenstern had need of English and English of Mor-
genstern, for after reading Lewis Carroll, Hillaire Belloc
(whose elegant savagery seems to owe much to Wilhelm
Busch), and sundry collections of light verse, I felt the
safe but dull ground of sense and logic swim deliciously
under me, in the happiest Morgensternian way. At Ox-
ford, I tried to interest an Oriel friend and editor of a po-
etry magazine, Alan Hodge, and through him his mentor,
Robert Graves, in starting an anthology of the *Galgen-
lieder* in English. This did not get off the ground at the
time, partly because, when visiting me in Poland, Alan
lost Morgenstern's trail in favor of that of the brilliant Pol-
ish poet, Julian Tuwim, and partly because I was too
diffident to continue on my own. I did draft about ten of
my favorite (and most easily rendered) *Galgenlieder* in
longhand and added to them in graduate school in
Warsaw. I was bemused to find these incunabula and some
Rilke translations, and very little else, intact in my
Nazi-ravaged digs after the German-Polish campaign in
1940. My place of birth being Istanbul, I was able to
acquire some Turkish papers and to bootleg the poems,
and myself, to Istanbul.

Neither service in the Office of Strategic Services
nor, later, a Ph.D. program in the United States were
conducive to emulating Morgenstern in English. In the
end, it was forty years since the rebirth of Poland in
1944–1945 before I was able to turn again to those
Oxonian palimpsests.

The would-be verse translator of the *Galgenlieder*
faces daunting difficulties on several levels. The purely
metric task of reproducing the easy play of iambics or

trochees, and the often saucy-to-brazen rhymes (for exam-
ple, *kommst / Bompst, / Dämmerung / Hämmerung,*
and so on) ask for some neologisms but are hardly more
demanding than those posed by any of the German or
Russian late romantics, who are prosodically conservative
except at moments of rhetorical passion—Goethe in
Ganymede and *Prometheus,* Lermontov *passim.* What is
more challenging, yet equally essential, is the teasing nar-
rative tone, the subtle lexical colorings drawing freely on
medieval, folksy, and bureaucratic language. One encoun-
ters mock solemnity throughout, the wide-eyed sincerity
garnishing less-than-plausible statements, and in the case
of suspected incredulity on the reader's part, sometimes
snappishness that takes one aback. The reader is asked to
swallow, *Im Inselwald zum stillen Kauz / da wohnt der
heilige Pardauz.* What, for all that is as mind-disturbing as
a Pre-Raffaelite painting, is an *Inselwald?* A forest on an
island? A patch of forest? It is, of course, just a bit of hazy
verbiage that conjures up an atmosphere of fairy tales
and the old-world language of the Brothers Grimm, in
whose *Stimmung* the poet hopes to get away with any-
thing. What is more, this intangible locus is speciously
pinpointed by the *zum* phrase, meaning that it is "under
the sign of" something, hence suggesting an inn, but
not a forest or an island. Worse yet, the eponymic *stiller
Kauz* designates a silent codger, recluse, or oddsbody,
or a spotted owl the size of Merlin's Archimedes. The
long-suffering reader is in doubt whether the mysterious
owlet (or codger) was roped in to rhyme with the nursery
word *Pardauz* (reaction to a loud crashing or tumbling
noise) or vice versa. In any case, a Saint Pardauz is a little
hard to take. The semantic farce of this is promptly en-
hanced by the author's sharp attack (this, too, unreal, of
course) on the reader's suspected incredulity. The reader,
to be sure, has not been able to utter a word and bears
the ensuing insults in silence—although silence was just
what enraged the testy teller.

Another of Morgenstern's artifices is his way of affirming or enhancing outlandish, mind-boggling statements by repeating them in a syntactic variant. Good examples are "The Ballgame," with its abstract yet disquieting nocturnal rustles. Elsewhere, as in "The Alum Tree," his comment on a charming but unheard-of proposition is *man glaubt es kaum* (you'd hardly credit it), as if the idea merely strained belief. The trick of solemnity by reiteration is redolent of biblical and other Semitic rhetoric, but not nineteenth-century prose styles. Still, most readers brought up in awareness of the New Testament remember that Jesus rode into Jerusalem "on an ass, the son of a she-ass."

A very "modern" mind-set of the "Songs from the Gallows" is revealed by the frequent note of derisive impatience with intrusive technology; even a century ago a young generation of environmentalists was growing up. Christian Morgenstern's native habitat is that of the pastoral—not that of the golf course and commuter train, but the meadows, where unicorns and hystrices and genies roam, as Palmström composes sneeze sonatas. No wonder the two friends have turned to "consumer-friendly" inventions like the Drivel-Shrivel (how this would deflate the press, the networks, and especially the sports commentators!). Less subversive, but comforting, are the two friendly clocks, the anecdote fitted with a time fuse, the Alps analyzed into tourists, cows, and igneous rock.

It is tempting to attribute the more philanthropic among the inventions to Palmström, subject as he is to "awe of the exalted," and the sterner and more abstract one to his fellow phantom, von Korf, who originally accompanied Palmström merely in the service of metric purity. Rhymes with Korf are "exceedingly rare," in the numismatist's phrase. In any case, the conjecture about stern Korf and gentle Palmström does not hold water (English metaphor; or proves *stichhaltig* [proof against jabs], German metaphor). As we may see, the vindication of ancient metaphors by vivisection and revival is another of Morgenstern's incidental airs and graces.

The gifted amateur linguist Richard Lederer writes that "analyzing [his] fantasies is like trying to dissect a soap bubble; surely one source of their enduring appeal . . . is their special sense of wonder about language. . . . In his writing he created a magic show of words, words pulled out of hats, words sawed in half, words dancing in the air, words that disappear or show up in strange places and forms." Lederer here talks about Lewis Carroll; but had he known Morgenstern in German or English—conditions contrary to fact—he would have analyzed the two magicians' work in parallel.

Songs from
the Gallows

Galgenlieder

Part One

Before
Palmström

The Moonsheep

The moonsheep on a spacious clearing
Abides and bides the final shearing.
The moonsheep.

The moonsheep, having plucked a weed,
Ascends again its mountain mead.
The moonsheep.

The moonsheep, dreaming, seems to face
Its self as universal space.
The moonsheep.

The moonsheep, lo, at dawn is dead.
Itself is white, the sun is red.
The moonsheep.

Das Mondschaf

Das Mondschaf steht auf weiter Flur.
Es harrt und harrt der großen Schur.
Das Mondschaf.

Das Mondschaf rupft sich einen Halm
und geht dann heim auf seine Alm.
Das Mondschaf.

Das Mondschaf spricht zu sich im Traum:
‚Ich bin des Weltalls dunkler Raum.'
Das Mondschaf.

Das Mondschaf liegt am Morgen tot.
Sein Leib ist weiß, die Sonn ist rot.
Das Mondschaf.

Lunovis

Lunovis in planitie stat
Cultrumque magn' exspectitat.
Lunovis.

Lunovis herba rapta it
In montes unde cucurrit.
Lunovis.

Lunovis videt somnium
Se culmen rer' ess' omnium.
Lunovis.

Lunovis mane mortuumst.
Sol ruber atque it albumst.
Lunovis.

Morgenstern provided a brilliant Latin replica of his pseudo-metaphysical ditty—probably just for the amusement of the educated (now termed "elitists"). The comic effect is much enhanced by the Vulgar Latin elisions: *mortuumst* for *mortuum est, albumst* for *album est,* and so on.

————

The Funnels

There wander through the night two funnels.
Down the twin torsos' tapered tunnels
White moonbeams flow
their path upon,
Serenely glow
and so
on.

Die Trichter

Zwei Trichter wandeln durch die Nacht.
Durch ihres Rumpfs verengten Schacht
fließt weißes Mondlicht
still und heiter
auf ihren
Waldweg
u. s.
w.

Fish's Night Song

Fisches Nachtgesang

```
            —
         ‿     ‿
      —    —    —
   ‿    ‿    ‿    ‿
      —    —    —
   ‿    ‿    ‿    ‿
      —    —    —
   ‿    ‿    ‿    ‿
      —    —    —
   ‿    ‿    ‿    ‿
      —    —    —
         ‿     ‿
            —

      ―――――――
```

The Knee

A knee bestrides the earth alone,
It is a knee, that's all!
It is no tree! It is no stone!
It is a knee, that's all.

A soldier in a war was shot
Right, left, and all around.
The knee remained, of all the lot,
Miraculously sound.

And now it strides the earth alone.
It is a knee, that's all.
It is no tree, it is no stone.
It is a knee, that's all.

Das Knie

Ein Knie geht einsam durch die Welt.
Es ist ein Knie, sonst nichts!
Es ist kein Baum! Es ist kein Zelt!
Es ist ein Knie, sonst nichts.

Im Kriege ward einmal ein Mann
erschossen um und um.
Das Knie allein blieb unverletzt—
als wär's ein Heiligtum.

Seitdem geht's einsam durch die Welt.
Es ist ein Knie, sonst nichts.
Es ist kein Baum, es ist kein Zelt.
Es ist ein Knie, sonst nichts.

———

The Sigh

A sigh was skating on ice one night,
Of love and enchantment dreaming.
'Twas by the ramparts, and snow-white
The rampart roofs were gleaming.

The sigh remembered a maiden sweet
And stopped, and stood aglow.
The ice sheet melted beneath its feet—
It sank, and was seen no mo'.

Der Seufzer

Ein Seufzer lief Schlittschuh auf nächtlichem Eis
und träumte von Liebe und Freude.
Es war an dem Stadtwall, und schneeweiß
glänzten die Stadtwallgebäude.

Der Seufzer dacht an ein Maidelein
und blieb erglühend stehen.
Da schmolz die Eisbahn unter ihm ein—
und er sank—und ward nimmer gesehen.

Ding, Dong, Bong

A solidary DONG-note rings
this night his manly knell;
In vestments Catholic he wings
High over hill and dell.

He searches for his belle-note DING,
who flew ahead of him;
but she has been philandering—
the outlook is quite grim.

"Come back, o give a ring, my DING,
DONG cares for you so dearly;
Come back, o DING, you lovesome thing,
Your DONG loves you sincerely!"

But DING, I must confide to you,
has pledged herself to BONG;
he is an upright Christian too
(which just inflames the wrong).

Still DONG keeps winging through the night
high over wood and rye;
but all in vain, alas! His flight
Is far off course, that's why.

Bim, Bam, Bum

Ein Glockenton fliegt durch die Nacht,
als hätt' er Vogelflügel;
er fliegt in römischer Kirchentracht
wohl über Tal und Hügel.

Er sucht die Glockentönin BIM,
die ihm vorausgeflogen;
d. h., die Sache ist sehr schlimm,
sie hat ihn nämlich betrogen.

10

,O komm,' so ruft er, ,komm, dein BAM
erwartet dich voll Schmerzen.
Komm wieder, BIM, geliebtes Lamm,
dein BAM liebt dich von Herzen!'

Doch BIM, daß ihr's nur alle wißt,
hat sich dem BUM ergeben;
der ist zwar auch ein guter Christ,
allein das ist es eben.

Der BAM fliegt weiter durch die Nacht
wohl über Wald und Lichtung.
Doch, ach, er fliegt umsonst! Das macht,
er fliegt in falscher Richtung.

The chase of bell notes seems to be a meditation on the ir-
reversibility of the Protestant Reformation. Is Bing the
united Protestant church of the future, eluding the Counter-
Reformationary Dong? Or merely a campanological wolf?

The Euphonic Mutt
A chow-chow
Went bow-wow
To a Mau-Mau.
Can you think why?
The Mooncalf leaked it to me:
The oversubt-
le mutt
Did it for rhymes, you see.

Das æsthetische Wiesel
Ein Wiesel
saß auf einem Kiesel
inmitten Bachgeriesel.

Wißt Ihr
weshalb?

Das Mondkalb
verriet es mir
im Stillen:

Das raffinier-
te Tier
tat's um des Reimes willen

The Worm's Confession

A worm which, barely extant,
lives in a shell at sea
in confidential accents
has bared his heart to me.

How it was pulsing, wheezing,
his piteous little heart!
You think that I am teasing?
Try not to be so smart.

A worm which, barely extant,
lives in a shell at sea
in confidential accents
did bare his heart to me.

Die Beichte des Wurms

Es lebt in einer Muschel
ein Wurm gar seltner Art;
der hat mir mit Getuschel
sein Herze offenbart.

Sein armes kleines Herze,
hei, wie das flog und schlug!
Ihr denket wohl, ich scherze?
Ach, denket nicht so klug.

Es lebt in einer Muschel
ein Wurm gar seltner Art;
der hat mir mit Getuschel
sein Herze offenbart.

———————

The Midnight Mouse

When gloom has gloamed and moon nor star
Inhabit heaven's chambers far,
Twelve times betrips the heavenly house
The midnight mouse.

It whistles on its little snout;
The slumbrous hell-nag whinnies out . . .
But calmly there patrols the house
The midnight mouse.

Its lord, you see, the Great White Knight,
Is out of town on such a night.
All's well with him. There guards his house
The midnight mouse.

Die Mitternachtsmaus

Wenn's mitternächtigt und nicht Mond
noch Stern das Himmelshaus bewohnt,
läuft zwölfmal durch das Himmelshaus
die Mitternachtsmaus.

Sie pfeift auf ihrem kleinen Maul,—
im Traume brüllt der Höllengaul . . .
Doch ruhig läuft ihr Pensum aus
die Mitternachtsmaus.

Ihr Herr, der große weiße Geist,
ist nämlich solche Nacht verreist.
Wohl ihm! Es hütet ihm sein Haus
die Mitternachtsmaus

The Cultist

A pike, converted by St. An-
tony, resolved with wife and son
to look to vegetarian thought
for moral uplift and support.

He ate henceforward only this:
Beach grass, beach lily, and beach grits.
But grass, grits, lily, Saints forfend!
Oozed grossly out the other end.

The entire pond was soiled and pussed,
Five hundred fishes bit the dust.
But St. Antonius' verdict was:
"A holy, holy, holy cause!"

Der Hecht

Ein Hecht, vom heiligen Antōn
bekehrt, beschloß, samt Frau und Sohn,
am vegetarischen Gedanken
moralisch sich emporzuranken.

Er aß seit jenem nur noch dies:
Seegras, Seerose und Seegrieß.
Doch Grieß, Gras, Rose floß, o Graus,
entsetzlich wieder hinten aus.

Der ganze Teich ward angesteckt.
Fünfhundert Fische sind verreckt.
Doch Sankt Antōn, gerufen eilig,
sprach nichts als: ‚Heilig! heilig! heilig!'

This melancholy tale may contain a warning for those on the
verge of being born again or lured into a diet of potassium
cyanide.

The Two Donkeys

A gloomy ass one morning said
Unto his mate of board and bed:

"I am so dumb, you are so dumb,
Let us seek death together, come!"

As it turned out (and often will),
The two are blithely living still.

Die beiden Esel

Ein finstrer Esel sprach einmal
zu seinem ehlichen Gemahl:

‚Ich bin so dumm, du bist so dumm,
wir wollen sterben gehen, kumm!‘

Doch wie es kommt so öfter eben:
Die beiden blieben fröhlich leben.

Suicidal impulses, fortunately or otherwise, tend to be
transient.

Water

Water's dumb, water's dumb,
Ever streaming, keeping mum;
Were it not, were it not,
It would utter nothing but:

Bread and beer, love and bliss—
Topics far from novel—this
Goes to show, goes to show,
Silent water's better so.

Das Wasser

Ohne Wort, ohne Wort
rinnt das Wasser immerfort;
andernfalls, andernfalls
spräch es doch nichts andres als:

Bier und Brot, Lieb und Treu,—
und das wäre auch nicht neu.
Dieses zeigt, dieses zeigt,
daß das Wasser besser schweigt.

———

The Air

The Air once threatened to expire.

"Oh, help me, help, celestial Sire,"
She cried with sadly clouded gaze;
"I'm stupid, torpid, in a daze,
You always know a way, Papa,
Send me on cruises, to a spa,
Sour milk is counseled for the skin . . .
If not—I'll call the Devil in!"

The Lord, not to be shamed by Air,
Invented "sound massage" for her.

We've had since then the world that SCREAMS.
And Air just rolls in it and beams.

Die Luft

Die Luft war einst dem Sterben nah.

‚Hilf mir, mein himmlischer Papa,‘
So rief sie mit sehr trübem Blick,
‚Ich werde dumm, ich werde dick;
Du weißt ja sonst für alles Rat—
Schick mich auf Reisen, in eine Bad,
Auch saure Milch wird gern empfohlen;—
Wenn nicht—laß ich den Teufel holen!‘

Der Herr, sich scheuend vor Blamage,
Erfand für sie die—Tonmassage.

Es gibt seitdem die Welt, die—schreit.
Wobei die Luft famos gedeiht.

"Lass ich den Teufel holen" is a neat evasion of the common
curse "Dich soll der Teufel holen" (May the Devil take you),
avoiding sacrilege.

18

The Board Fence
There was a wooden fence I knew
With intervals for looking through.

An architect who passed this way
Turned up before it one fine day,

Took out the spaces, hem by hem,
And built a handsome house of them.

The fence just lingered on, a rump
Of planks and nothing, like a chump.

A sight to sicken man and horse;
The City pulled it down, of course.

The architect absconded, though,
To Afri- or Americo.

Der Lattenzaun
Es war einmal ein Lattenzaun
mit Zwischenraum, hindurchzuschaun.

Ein Architekt, der dieses sah,
stand eines Tages plötzlich da

und nahm den Zwischenraum heraus
und baute draus ein großes Haus.

Der Zaun hingegen stand ganz dumm
Mit Latten ohne was herum.

Ein Anblick gräßlich und gemein;
Drum zog ihn der Senat auch ein.

Der Architekt jedoch entfloh
Nach Afri- od Ameriko.

The architect's detached view registers the boards and the slots merely as complementary contributors to the visual image of the fences. He chooses the more colorful ones, the interstices, to build with. This poem is vintage Morgenstern, and proverbial in German.

The Two Bottles

Two bottles stand upon a stump,
The one is slim, the other plump.
They'd like to marry now,
But who can tell them how?

The couple, night and noon,
Binocularly moon
To heavens blue or mottled,
But no one bustles doon
To get them interbottled.

Die beiden Flaschen

Zwei Flaschen stehn auf einer Bank,
die eine dick, die andre schlank.
Sie möchten gerne heiraten.
Doch wer soll ihnen beiraten?

Mit ihrem Doppel-Auge leiden
sie auf zum blauen Firmament . . .
Doch niemand kommt herabgerennt
und kopuliert die beiden.

———

The Lay of the Khaki Cork

A khaki cork on a lacquered shelf
Stands mirrored; yet, agree,
It could not ever see itself
(assuming it could see).

For the reflection is, my love,
Coaxial with its course.
If you incline it, the above
No longer holds, of course.

If we perchance were mirrored, men,
In—let us say, in space!
And upright—would we not be then
In quite analogous case?

Das Lied vom blonden Korken

Ein blonder Korke spiegelt sich
in einem Lacktablett—
allein er säh sich dennoch nich,
selbst wenn er Augen hätt'!

Das macht, dieweil er senkrecht steigt
zu seinem Spiegelbild!
Wenn man ihn freilich seitwärts neigt,
zerfällt, was oben gilt.

O Mensch, gesetzt, du spiegelst dich
im, sagen wir,—im All!
Und senkrecht!—wärest du dann nich
ganz in demselben Fall?

One of Morgenstern's bemusing so-what poems.

———

22

The Die

A die complained: "I have not been
Quite comfortable in my skin.

Of my six planes, the sitting side,
And bore it but my single mark,
Must ever gaze, not far and wide,
But into earth's eternal dark."

When earth beneath him heard the cube,
She very nearly blew a tube.

"You jackass," said she, "what a farce!
I'm dark when covered by your arse!
As soon as you will move the same,
I'll shine as with a gem-like flame."

The die, insulted past repair,
Chose not to bandy words with her.

Der Würfel

Ein Würfel sprach zu sich: ,Ich bin
mir selbst nicht völlig zum Gewinn!

Denn meines Wesens sechste Seite,
und sei es auch Ein Auge bloß,
sieht immerdar, statt in die Weite,
der Erde ewig dunklen Schoß.'

Als dies die Erde, drauf er ruhte,
vernommen, ward ihr schlimm zumute.

,Du Esel,' sprach sie, ,ich bin dunkel,
weil dein Gesäß mich just bedeckt!

Ich bin so licht wie ein Karfunkel,
sobald du dich hinweggefleckt.ʻ

Der Würfel, innerlichst beleidigt,
hat sich nicht weiter drauf verteidigt.

———

The Old and Young Pretenders

"I am Count Réaumur, you scum,
And hate you like ten plagues!
Go serve that Celsius, be dumb,
You rotten renegades!"

King Fahrenheit, back in his nook,
Spooned up his grits and ale.
"Ah—how I loved it when they took
Their readings by my scale!"

Kronprätendenten

—,Ich bin der Graf von Réaumur
und haß euch wie die Schande!
Dient nur dem Celsio für und für,
ihr Apostatenbande!'

Im Winkel König Fahrenheit
hat still sein Mus gegessen.
—,Ach Gott, sie war doch schön, die Zeit,
die man nach mir gemessen!'

The Réaumur scale gradually fell out of use early in this cen-
tury. The Fahrenheit scale, with its quaint disregard of water,
steam, and ice, was espoused by the English-speaking countries
in order to further complicate the calculations already be-
deviled by the foot/pound/second system. Elsewhere King
Fahrenheit is a mummy.

———

Oirish Flood

The waters swirled, the waters biled
The whole berluddy world was riled;
The town was bogged,
The owl was logged,
And on the oaktree sat a choild.

Its little feet are getting wet,
It cries: "The wat-, the wat-, no let!"
O'Whalefish beams
And says: "Meseems
The waters haven't crested yet."

The water flowed with rush and swish,
The earth became a water dish.
And choild and owl,
Oh murder foul,
Were glugglugged by O'Whalefafish.

Der Walfafisch
oder das Überwasser

Das Wasser rinnt, das Wasser spinnt,
bis es die ganze Welt gewinnt.
Das Dorf ersäuft,
die Eule läuft,
und auf der Eiche sitzt ein Kind.

Dem Kind sind schon die Beinchen naß,
es ruft: ,Das Wass, das Wass, das Wass!'
Der Walfisch weint
und sagt: ,Mir scheint,
es regnet ohne Unterlaß.'

Das Wasser rann mit Zasch und Zisch,
die Erde ward zum Wassertisch.
  Und Kind und Eul,
    o Greul, o Greul—
sie frissifraß der Walfafisch.

———

The Nasodary

Upon its nose's soles
The nasodary strides;
A grown one with two foals.
It's yet unclassified.

It's missing from the tissues
Of Webst- or -tannica.
Fresh from my lyre now issues
Its being's avatar.

Said nasodary, gliding
Upon its nose's soles,
Has ever since been striding
Escorted by its foals.

Das Nasobēm

Auf seinen Nasen schreitet
einher das Nasobēm,
von seinem Kind begleitet.
Es steht noch nicht im Brehm.

Es steht noch nicht im Meyer.
Und auch im Brockhaus nicht.
Es trat aus meiner Leyer
zum ersten Mal ans Licht.

Auf seinen Nasen schreitet
(wie schon gesagt) seitdem,
von seinem Kind begleitet,
einher das Nasobēm.

Meyer and *Brockhaus* were the most authoritative "conversation dictionaries" of the time. *Brehm* refers to *Brehms Tierleben,* a multivolume zoological reference work.

Antology

The Gig-ant was in Nature's annals
The largest of terrestrial mammals.

(Gig was a number without rival,
Too astronomic for survival.)

Where is its realm? Where is itself?
Pale bones on a museum shelf!—

Flanked by a much diminished pendant,
The Twelefant, its late descendant,

Which waned as slowly as it grew;
For time was cheap, and numbers too.

At last a timid prairie-rover,
The tiny Elefant, took over.

But Man, all drunk with rifle-musk,
And lusting for its precious tusk,

Shoots it—a crass impediment
To the next Tenant's due descent.

S.P.C.A., oh, stop him, sue him!
Oh, do not suffer Man to ruin

The stages of this evolution,
That stately, leisured diminution!

Ah, how the ant will bless you, think,
For letting it live on and shrink,

Till wordlessly one distant day
The Nihilant will fade . . . away . . .

Anto-logie

Im Anfang lebte, wie bekannt,
als größter Säuger der Gig-ant.

Wobei gig eine Zahl ist, die
es nicht mehr gibt,—so groß war sie!

Doch jene Größe schwand wie Rauch.
Zeit gab's genug—und Zahlen auch.

Bis eines Tags, ein winzig Ding,
der Zwölef-ant das Reich empfing.

Wo blieb sein Reich? Wo blieb er selb?—
Sein Bein wird im Museum gelb.

Zwar gab die gütige Natur
den Elef-anten uns dafur.

Doch ach, der Pulverpavian,
der Mensch, voll Gier nach seinem Zahn,

erschießt ihn, statt ihm Zeit zu lassen,
zum Zehen-anten zu verblassen.

O Klub zum Schutz der wilden Tiere,
hilf, daß der Mensch nicht ruiniere

die Sprossen dieser Riesenleiter,
die stets noch weiter führt und weiter!

Wie dankbar wird der Ant dir sein,
läßt du ihn wachsen und gedeihn,—

bis er dereinst im Nebel hinten
als Nulel-ant wird stumm verschwinden.

———

The Hystrix

The great East-Asian porcupine
(Hystrix grotei Kurtz),
The great East-Asian porcupine
From Indonesia, hurts.

If in the jungle you should stray
Upon its quiet rounds,
It may abruptly step, they say,
Quite out of nature's bounds.

Then fury goads it so, behold,
That ere you can exclaim,
It shoots its quills, both young and old,
Into your shrinking frame.

Festooned in spikes from crop to can
You stand against a tree,
An instant St. Sebastian,
Amazed at what you see.

Whereas the hystrix leaves the scene,
Unstrung in soul and bones,
And in a jungle lair unseen
Atones.

Die Hystrix

Das hinterindische Stachelschwein
(hystrix grotei Gray),
das hinterindische Stachelschwein
aus Siam, das tut weh.

Entdeckst du wo im Walde drauß
bei Siam seine Spur,
dann tritt es manchmal, sagt man, aus
den Schranken der Natur.

Dann gibt sein Zorn ihm so Gewalt,
daß, eh du dich versiehst,
es seine Stacheln jung und alt
auf deinen Leib verschießt.

Von oben bis hinab sodann
stehst du gespickt am Baum,
ein heiliger Sebastian,
und traust den Augen kaum.

Die Hystrix aber geht hinweg,
an Leib und Seele wüst.
Sie sitzt im Dschungel im Versteck
und büßt.

The zoological label of the Hystrix is as plausible and spurious
as is its painful (to both target and launcher) shower of darts.

Testing

For a unique experiment
I bought a needle-book, then spent

Some more upon a worn but very
High-spirited old dromedary.

A man of substance joined the lists,
With bags of gold in both his fists.

The rich man now essayed his fate
And knocked upon the pearly gate.

St. Peter boomed: "The gospels show
That sooner shall a camel go,

Aye, through a needle's eye, than you
Shall walk these spacious portals through."

I, strong in faith as any priest,
Encouraging my humpbacked beast,

Held up behind the needle's hole
A scrumptious little sugar roll.

And cross my heart—the brute went through!
With fearsome writhings, it is true.

The rich man merely stared, aghast,
And slowly whispered: "All is lost."

Die Probe

Zu einem seltsamen Versuch
erstand ich mir ein Nadelbuch.

Und zu dem Buch ein altes zwar,
doch äußerst kühnes Dromedar.

Ein Reicher auch daneben stand,
zween Säcke Gold in jeder Hand.

Der Reiche ging alsdann herfür
und klopfte an die Himmelstür.

Drauf Petrus sprach: ‚Geschrieben steht,
daß ein Kamel weit eher geht

durchs Nadelöhr als du, du Heid,
durch diese Türe groß und breit!'

Ich, glaubend fest an Gottes Wort,
ermunterte das Tier sofort,

ihm zeigend hinterm Nadelöhr
ein Zuckerhörnchen als Douceur.

Und in der Tat! Das Vieh ging durch,
obzwar sich quetschend wie ein Lurch!

Der Reiche aber sah ganz stier
und sagte nichts als: ‚Wehe mir!'

Does this parable not contain a crucial flaw? If a camel sup-
posedly would pass through a needle's eye more readily than a
rich man could enter the pearly gate, and the camel *does* pass,
does not the rich man's chance improve?

———

By the Year Ten Thousand

Ants—more quaintly "emmets" named—
Are so smart now they have tamed
Chamois of the alpine peaks
To improve on their physiques.

Being very much the smaller,
And the chamois so much taller,
They use one (or two sometimes)
To assist on mountain climbs.

When an aerie they have found
Has been scavenged to the ground,
And the angry aquila
Calls for myrmecophaga,

They will quit his nest and coat
And ascend their mountain goat,
Which by ricocheting leaps
Bears them to their native heaps.

Tethered there, the chamois pace—
Helots of the formic race—
By the teeming aphid clusters,
Breathing curses at their masters.

Im Jahre 19000

Die Ameisen oder Emsen
sind so weit jetzt, daß sie Gemsen
sich als Sklaven halten (aus
Gründen ihres Körperbaus).

Da sie selber sehr viel kleiner,
so bedienen sie sich einer
Gemse oder zweier Gemsen
zu Gebirgspartien, die Emsen.

Ist sodann ein Adlernest
abgesucht bis auf den Rest,
gehn sie endlich, zog der Weih
schon den Ameisbären bei,

wieder ihm aus Horst und Rock—
und besteigen ihren Bock,
der sie, wie ein Stein, der springt,
heim zu ihrem Hügel bringt.

Angepflöckt, so stehn die Gemsen
in der Nähe dort der Emsen,
bei den Läusen u. s. w.
und verwünschen ihre Reiter.

_____

The Gi . . . ant . . . Turtle

I am a thousand seasons old
And daily gather age;
The Vandal chieftain Thiubold
First reared me in a cage.

Since then a lot has come to be,
But I know nothing of it;
A merchant now exhibits me
At Fredericksburg for profit.

What mortals suffer passed me by,
And death's black wreath of myrtle:
I am the gi . . . I am the gi . . .
I am the gi . . . ant . . . turtle.

Die Schildkrökröte

Ich bin nun tausend Jahre alt
und werde täglich älter;
der Gotenkönig Theobald
erzog mich im Behälter.

Seitdem ist mancherlei geschehn,
doch weiß ich nichts davon;
zur Zeit, da läßt für Geld mich sehn
ein Kaufmann zu Heilbronn.

Ich kenne nicht des Todes Bild
und nicht des Sterbens Nöte:
Ich bin die Schild—ich bin die Schild—
ich bin die Schild—krö—kröte.

These giant turtles, right-wing to begin with, tend to become
comatose in old age.

———————

Gull Song

The gulls all look to me as if
They bore the name of Alice.
They may be seen on surf and cliff
And killed with shot and malice.

I do not shoot the seagulls dead,
I rather let them be.
I feed them crumbs of gingerbread
And nuts of Barbary.

You'll never equal, Man, at best
The soaring seagull's semblance;
So if your name be Alice, rest
Content with that resemblance.

Möwenlied

Die Möwen sehen alle aus,
als ob sie Emma hießen.
Sie tragen einen weißen Flaus
und sind mit Schrot zu schießen.

Ich schieße keine Möwe tot,
ich laß sie lieber leben—
und füttre sie mit Roggenbrot
und rötlichen Zibeben.

O Mensch, du wirst nie nebenbei
der Möwe Flug erreichen.
Wofern du Emma heißest, sei
zufrieden, ihr zu gleichen.

Alice suggests itself as a more nondescript and gullsome name
than the original's Emma—no doubt partly owing to Jane
Austen.

Roots

Two roots of hemlock, gnarled and hoar,
Hold converse on the forest floor.

What gossip wafts from crown to crown
They here communicate deep down.

A grizzled squirrel sits and taps,
Crocheting socks for them, perhaps.

One might say: kniggh, the other: kneagh.
And that will do it for a deagh.

Die zwei Wurzeln

Zwei Tannenwurzeln gross und alt
unterhalten sich im Wald.

Was droben in den Wipfeln rauscht,
das wird hier unten ausgetauscht.

Ein altes Eichhorn sitzt dabei
und strickt wohl Strümpfe für die zwei.

Die eine sagt: knig. Die andre sagt: knag.
Das ist genug für einen Tag.

———

Part Two

Palmström
and
Korf

Palmström

Palmström stands beside a pond
And unfolds a crimson handkerchief, o look!
There's an oak tree pictured there, as by a wand
And a man with a book.

Palmström dare not blow his nose.
Think of him as one of those
Apt to be abruptly halted
By sheer awe of the exalted.

Gently he is seen refolding
What he only just unwrested;
And no man of sentiment will scold him
For departing still congested.

Palmström

Palmström steht an einem Teiche
und entfaltet groß ein rotes Taschentuch:
Auf dem Tuch ist eine Eiche
dargestellt sowie ein Mensch mit einem Buch.

Palmström wagt nicht, sich hineinzuschneuzen.—
Er gehört zu jenen Käuzen,
die oft unvermittelt-nackt
Ehrfurcht vor dem Schönen packt.

Zärtlich faltet er zusammen,
was er eben erst entbreitet.
Und kein Fühlender wird ihn verdammen,
weil er ungeschneuzt entschreitet.

This poem has been subtitled "The Birth of Esthetics," for
what "halted" Palmström was surely an intimation of the sub-
lime, whether purveyed by a cotton hanky, or by turning a cor-

ner at the Vatican Museum, or by coming across some of
Picasso's *disiecta membra*.

The irony which seems to pervade this poem sounds like a
cheap thrust at lowbrow taste—but Palmström, our arbiter, is
himself bowled over by the hanky's esthetic revelation.

————————

Village in Thrace

Palmström travels, with a Baron Korf,
To a town in Thrace called Xenomorph.

All he hears—first, last, and interim—
Stays incomprehensible to him.

Baron Korf as well (who joined the spree
For the rhyme's sake) finds, "it's Greek to me."

But this very ignorance is bliss!
Palmström homes, quite pale with happiness.

With his diary he lives anew
"An experience sweet as honeydew."

Das böhmische Dorf

Palmström reist, mit einem Herrn von Korf,
in ein sogenanntes böhmisches Dorf.

Unverständlich bleibt ihm alles dort,
von dem ersten bis zum letzten Wort.

Auch von Korf, der nur des Reimes wegen
ihn begleitet, ist um Rat verlegen.

Doch grad dieses macht ihn blass vor Glück.
Tief entzückt kehrt unser Freund zurück.

Und er schreibt in seine Wochenchronik:
Wieder ein Erlebnis voll von Honig.

———

Nor'ard

Palmström's pulses have been racing;
Now he slumbers nor'ward-facing.

For an eastward, westward, so'th'ard
Slumber means your heart is smothered.

(Those are temperate-region data,
Not for use near the equator.)

Doctors proved this true on chickens
And persuaded even Dickens

That the earth's magnetic forces
Are what sets our beds' true courses.

Palmström, ever thinking forward,
Moves his bed and points it nor'ward.

And, asleep, not seldom—hark!
Hears the arctic fox's bark.

Nach Norden

Palmström ist nervös geworden;
darum schläft er jetzt nach Norden.

Denn nach Osten, Westen, Süden
schlafen, heißt das Herz ermüden.

(Wenn man nämlich in Europen
lebt, nicht südlich in den Tropen.)

Solches steht bei zwei Gelehrten,
die auch Dickens schon bekehrten—

und erklärt sich aus dem steten
Magnetismus des Planeten.

Palmström also heilt sich örtlich,
nimmt sein Bett und stellt es nördlich.

Und im Traum, in einigen Fällen,
hört er den Polarfuchs bellen.

A new medico-quackish fad was launched in Germany every ten years or so, mostly to produce sleep, hair, bosoms, potency, muscles, or slimness by the action of zodiac signs, magnetic fields, or herb decoctions. Palmström is more successful than most.

———————

Sleep before Midnight

Supervised by twelve hypnologists,
Palmström sleeps the famous "sleep before midnight"
to attest its healthful properties.

At the stroke of twelve as he wakes up,
lo! the scientists are heavy-lidded;
he alone is frisky as a playful pup.

Der vorgeschlafene Heilschlaf

Palmström schläft vor zwölf Experten
den berühmten ‚Schlaf vor Mitternacht',
seine Heilkraft zu erhärten.

Als er, da es zwölf, erwacht,
sind die zwölf Experten sämtlich müde.
Er allein ist frisch wie eine junge Rüde!

The Ball Game

Palmström takes some paper from his drawer
And distributes it about the floor.

Having formed it into many a ball,
Having deftly scattered them at evenfall.

So he deftly sows the spheres (packed tight)
That if he perchance wake up at night,

That if he should wake at night, he might
Hear them rustle, and a creepy fright

Might assault him (that at night a crawly fright
Might assault him) at the crawl of balls packed tight.

Die Kugeln

Palmström nimmt Papier aus seinem Schube.
Und verteilt es kunstvoll in der Stube.

Und nachdem er Kugeln draus gemacht.
Und verteilt es kunstvoll, und zur Nacht.

Und verteilt die Kugeln so (zur Nacht),
daß er, wenn er plötzlich nachts erwacht,

daß'er, wenn er nachts erwacht, die Kugeln
knistern hört und ihn ein heimlich Grugeln

packt (daß ihn dann nachts ein heimlich Grugeln
packt) beim Spuk der packpapiernen Kugeln . . .

Bona Fide

Palmström roams an unfamiliar town . . .
What a downpour, he remarks, I do declare!
And he tilts his collar up and bowler down.

Yet aloft is clear and placid air,
And no zephyr turns a leaf around.
His conclusion, though, is only fair:

For the pavement which the stranger paces
Has been—speckled by a crafty Council.
(One of bona fide's shakier cases).

Bona Fide

Palmström geht durch eine fremde Stadt . . .
Lieber Gott, so denkt er, welch ein Regen!
Und er spannt den Schirm auf, den er hat.

Doch am Himmel tut sich nichts bewegen,
und kein Windhauch rührt ein Blatt.
Gleichwohl darf man jenen Argwohn hegen.

Denn das Pflaster, über das er wandelt,
ist vom Magistrat voll List—gesprenkelt.
Bona fide hat der Gast gehandelt.

———

Animal Costumes
Palmström likes portraying animals
And is training two young tailors to produce
Only animal costumes.

Thus he likes at times to hunker as a raven
On the topmost branches of an oak,
And observe the sky.

Often as a St. Bernard he will
Lower shaggy head on valiant paws,
Bark in his sleep and dream of rescued climbers.

Or he'll weave a net in his backyard
Out of string and sit in it for days
As a spider.

Or he'll swim, a goggle-gloating carp,
Round and round the fountain in his pond
And permit the kids to feed him.

Or he hangs, accoutered as a stork,
From a dirigible's cabin
On a trip to Egypt.

Im Tierkostüm
Palmström liebt es, Tiere nachzuahmen,
und erzieht zwei junge Schneider
lediglich auf Tierkostüme.

So z. B. hockt er gern als Rabe
auf dem oberen Aste einer Eiche
und beobachter den Himmel.

Häufig auch als Bernhardiner
legt er zottigen Kopf auf tapfere Pfoten,
bellt im Schlaf und träumt gerettete Wanderer.

Oder spinnt ein Netz in seinem Garten
aus Spagat und sitzt als eine Spinne
tagelang in dessen Mitte.

Oder schwimmt, ein glotzgeäugter Karpfen,
rund um die Fontäne seines Teiches
und erlaubt den Kindern ihn zu füttern.

Oder hängt sich im Kostüm des Storches
unter eines Luftschiffs Gondel
und verreist so nach Ägypten.

———

The Korf Clock

Korf invents a kind of clock
Fitted with diverging hands,
Whose rotation breaks the lock
Of a uniform advance.

When it's three, it's also nine,
When it's four, it's also eight;
Just a glance will undermine
Time's despotic forward gait.

By its pointing Janus-minded
Fore and aft upon its shelf
(This is why he has designed it)
Time must cancel out itself.

Die Korfsche Uhr

Korf erfindet eine Uhr,
die mit zwei Paar Zeigern kreist
und damit nach vorn nicht nur,
sondern auch nach rückwärts weist.

Zeigt sie zwei,—somit auch zehn;
zeigt sie drei,—somit auch neun;
und man braucht nur hinzusehn,
um die Zeit nicht mehr zu scheun.

Denn auf dieser Uhr von Korfen
mit dem januschaften Lauf
(dazu ward sie so entworfen):
hebt die Zeit sich selber auf.

———

Palmström's Clock

Palmström's clock displays, in turn,
A mimosa-like concern.

He who begs its intervention
May be sure of kind attention:

Frequently it has responded
As petitioners have wanted,

Raced ahead some hours, or waited,
As its sympathy dictated.

Though a clock, it has no patience
With dogmatic regulations:

Works like others', part for part:
Palmström's has a feeling heart.

Palmströms Uhr

Palmströms Uhr ist andrer Art,
reagiert mimosisch zart.

Wer sie bittet, wird empfangen.
Oft schon ist sie so gegangen,

wie man herzlich sie gebeten,
ist zurück- und vorgetreten,

eine Stunde, zwei, drei Stunden,
je nachdem sie mitempfunden.

Selbst als Uhr, mit ihren Zeiten,
will sie nicht Prinzipien reiten:

Zwar ein Werk, wie allerwärts,
doch zugleich ein Werk—mit Herz.

Korf's Olfaction

Korf's olfaction is uncanny.
But the common man's is weak.
Their "can't smell a thing" has many
Times propelled him up a creek.

Like Stendhal (see Henri Beyle)
He records, with feelings blended:
It will take a monstrous while
Till at length I'm comprehended.

Korfs Geruchsinn

Korfs Geruchsinn ist enorm.
Doch der Nebenwelt gebrichts!—
und ihr Wort: ‚Wir riechen nichts‛,
bringt ihn oft aus aller Form.

Und er schreibt wie Stendhal Beyle
stumm in sein Notizbuch ein:
Einst, nach überlanger Weile,
werde ich verstanden sein.

———

Palmström to a Nightingale Who Robs Him of Sleep
Would you turn into a fish for me
And adapt yourself to this acoustic'ly?
Failing which, it is absurd
To expect that slumber's gentle pall
Sink on me, which I have need of after all!
Do it, if a noble bird!

It will hardly cool your mate's devotion
When in veritable flounder motion
You will flap the air, or treetop leisure savor,
Or, a catfish winged, your pliant feeler
Waft about him, gracious Philomela,
(who will surely do me that small favor!)

Palmström an eine Nachtigall, die ihn nicht schlafen ließ
Möchtest du dich nicht in einen Fisch verwandeln
und gesanglich dementsprechend handeln?
da es sonst unmöglich ist,
daß mir unternachts des Schlafes Labe
blüht, die ich nun doch notwendig habe!
Tu es, wenn du edel bist!

Deine Frau im Nest wird dich auch so bewundern,
wenn du gänzlich in der Art der Flundern
auftrittst und im Wipfel wohlig ruhst
oder, eine fliegende Makrele,
sie umflatterst, holde Philomele
(—die du mir gewiß die Liebe tust!).

The Coat at Night

The coat, worn in the daytime, lies
At rest within the night-dark house;
Through its vacated sleeves there plies
The mouse.

All through its hollow sleeves there plies
In ghostly to and fro the mouse . . .
The coat, worn in the daytime, lies
At rest within the house.

Day-worn, within the silent house
In night's dark lap it dozes,
And, tunneled by its faithful mouse,
Reposes.

Der Rock

Der Rock, am Tage angehabt,
er ruht zur Nacht sich schweigend aus;
durch seine hohlen Ärmel trabt
die Maus.

Durch seine hohlen Ärmel trabt
gespenstisch auf und ab die Maus . . .
Der Rock, am Tage angehabt,
er ruht zur Nacht sich aus.

Er ruht, am Tage angehabt,
im Schoß der Nacht sich schweigend aus,
er ruht, von seiner Maus durchtrabt,
sich aus.

———

Alpinism

>Korf seeks to arrive (while Palmström helps)
>at the cubic volume of the Alps;
>thinking them an isometric block
>wrought of tourists, cows, and igneous rock.
>Its mean altitude, he soon decides,
>Comes to forty miles, like all the sides.
>Saving travel, mentally he might
>climb the surface on a sultry night . . .
>Forty miles above the Havel's mists
>He is awed by stars the size of fists.

Alpinismus

>Palmström rechnet mit v. Korf zu Haus
>den Kubikinhalt der Alpen aus
>(denn er denkt die Alpen sich als einen
>Würfel aus Touristen, Kühn u. Steinen)
>und fixiert des Würfels Höh auf praeter
>propter 63 Kilometer.
>Er besteigt, statt daß wie sonst er reist,
>ihn in Julinächten oft im Geist.
>190 000 Fuß ob Tschirne
>liegt er und sieht faustgroß die Gestirne.

The Havel, Spree, and other opaque rivulets have meandered about the Slavic stronghold of Berlin since the seventh century. Before then, Berlin may have been a rest stop for the Gothic tribes on their way to Byzantium and Italy.

Korf's Drivel-Shrivel

Korf, who takes himself for model,
Likes his reading swift and spare;
Floods of coarse pretentious twaddle
Daily drive him to despair.

Solid sense for pleasing shape
Needs but six or seven words,
And the pompsters' plastic tape-
Worm of jargon's for the birds.

So he builds a tool whereby
The entangled mind is freed:
Scanning-glasses for the eye
Which condense the stuff they read!

Thus, these present rhymes the stark
Lenses would not even sight!
Thirty-seven of them might
Rate a single question-mark!!

Die Brille

Korf liest gerne schnell und viel;
darum widert ihn das Spiel
all des zwölfmal unerbetnen
Ausgewalzten, Breitgetretnen.

Meistes ist in sechs bis acht
Wörtern völlig abgemacht,
und in ebensoviel Sätzen
läßt sich Bandwurmweisheit schwätzen.

Es erfindet drum sein Geist
etwas, was ihn dem entreißt:
Brillen, deren Energien
ihm den Text—zusammenziehen!

Beispielsweise dies Gedicht
läse, so bebrillt, man—nicht!
Dreiunddreißig seinesgleichen
gäben erst—Ein—Fragezeichen!!

———

The Luncheon Gazette

Korf invents a lunchtime publication
which, when one has read one's fill,
one is full.

Quite without the preparation
of the least collateral collation,
no starch, no greens, no meat.
Everyone of any penetration
buys the sheet.

Die Mittagszeitung

Korf erfindet eine Mittagszeitung,
welche, wenn man sie gelesen hat,
ist man satt.

Ganz ohne Zubereitung
irgendeiner andern Speise.
Jeder auch nur etwas Weise
hält das Blatt.

The Alum Tree

Palmström has a capsule built for him,
which he fills with alum to the brim,
Then he scrupulously plants it out
in his yard and waits for it to sprout.

Sunbeams fall on it and sheets of rain,
and the earth accepts the alien grain,
taken in, or thinking: let's amuse
The old gent—what do I stand to lose?

So she thrusts from out the vessel's spout
A most graceful alum sulfate sprout!
And the spriglet grows, incredibly,
Into a prodigious alum tree!!

Humbly grateful for the magic stuff,
Palmström has the whole tree—gargled off!
And by anyone whose throat is sore:
No one's been so lionized before . . .

Der Alaunbaum

Palmström lässt sich eine Kugel baun
und erfüllt dieselbe mit Alaun.
Diese pflanzt er dann in seinem Garten,
um den Wuchs des Kornes abzuwarten.

Sonne scheint und Regen fällt darauf,
und die Erde nimmt das Korn in Kauf,
lässt sich täuschen oder denkt ,dem Mann
macht es Spass, und mir kommt's nicht drauf an.`

Und so treibt sie aus der Kapsel Hals
ein Alaunreis, zierlich und voll Salz.
Und das Reis erwächst, man glaubt es kaum,
Bis zu einem wundervollen Baum.

Palmström, ohne vor Triumph zu turkeln,
lässt den Baum von A bis Z—vergurgeln!
Und von jedermann, der Halsweh hat.
Palmström wird der Favorit der Stadt.

This demonstrates the close give-and-take between Palmström
and nature. One of the little buried jewels is the clause *man
glaubt es kaum* (you'd hardly believe it) for the reader's (but
not quite Palmström's) "Oh, come on, tell me another!" Sus-
pension of vulgar disbelief is, of course, a prime condition of
Galgenhood.

———

Delayed Action Jokes

Korf invents a kind of shaggy-dog tale
With its trigger set for hours ahead.
Everybody hears it with a yawn.

But as if a secret fuse had smoldered,
Deep at night you will abruptly waken,
Blithely bubbling like a brimful baby.

Korf erfindet eine Art von Witzen

Korf erfindet eine Art von Witzen,
die erst viele Stunden später wirken.
Jeder hört sie an mit Langeweile.

Doch als hätt' ein Zunder still geglommen,
wird man nachts im Bette plötzlich munter,
selig lächelnd wie ein satter Säugling.

———————

The Spaced-Out Watch
Every bedtime Palmström drops his watch
(So as not to hear its pesky ticking)
In a glass of opium or scotch.

Morning finds it spaced-out on its back;
And to bring it round alive and kicking,
He must rinse it with strong mocha (black).

Palmström legt des Nachts sein Chronometer—
Palmström legt des Nachts sein Chronometer,
um sein lästig Ticken nicht zu hören,
in ein Glas mit Opium oder Äther.

Morgens ist die Uhr dann ganz ‚herunter'.

Ihren Geist von neuem zu beschwören,
wäscht er sie mit schwarzem Mokka munter.

———

Heavy Air

Korf invents a form of indoor air
Corpulent enough for any
Object to be stuck therein.

Just for illustration, take the many
Times he had to down his pen,
Phoned or interrupted here or there—

Now he parks it in the atmosphere
(No one finding this uncanny),
In mid air, wherever, there or here.

Die Zimmerluft

Korf erfindet eine Zimmerluft,
die so korpulent, daß jeder
Gegenstand drin stecken bleibt.

Etwa mitten, wenn er mit dem Feder-
halter grade nicht mehr schreibt,
weil die Dienstmagd an die Türe pufft—

gibt er kurzweg ihm ein Alibi—
mitten in die Luft entweder
oder sonstwo in ihr, gleichviel wo und wie.

————

The Impossible Event

Palmström, middle-aged or over,
at a crossing marked "Pedestrian"
by a chariot multequestrian
is run over.

How, he wonders, calmly striving
and determinedly surviving,
did this accident befall?
Why, at that, occur at all?

Must one blame exalted stations
for deficient regulations?
Does a city ordnance say
drivers here have right-of-way?

Or was it the Law's instruction
here to bar the swift reduction
of live men to dead and halt?
In a word: who was at fault?

Swathed in towels but still seraphic,
he reviews the rules of traffic
and is fairly prompt in noting:
driving cars there was *verboten*.

And he comes to the conclusion
the event was an illusion,
for his reason's razor slant
rules: what must not happen, can't.

Die unmögliche Tatsache

Palmström, etwas schon an Jahren,
wird an einer Straßenbeuge
und von einem Kraftfahrzeuge
überfahren.

‚Wie war‘ (spricht er, sich erhebend
und entschlossen weiterlebend)
‚möglich, wie dies Unglück, ja—:
daß es überhaupt geschah?

Ist die Staatskunst anzuklagen
in bezug auf Kraftfahrwagen?
Gab die Polizeivorschrift
hier dem Fahrer freie Trift?

Oder war vielmehr verboten,
hier Lebendige zu Toten
umzuwandeln, —kurz und schlicht:
Durfte hier der Kutscher nicht—?‘

Eingehüllt in feuchte Tücher,
prüft er die Gesetzesbücher
und ist alsobald im klaren:
Wagen durften dort nicht fahren!

Und er kommt zu dem Ergebnis:
Nur ein Traum war das Erlebnis.
Weil, so schließt er messerscharf,
nicht sein kann, was nicht sein darf.

Wrong Address

Korf receives from high authority a five-
barreled armor-piercing questionnaire:
who he was, and why, how long alive,

Whom he owed allegiance heretofore,
if he was employed, in what, and where,
then, to whom, and to what end, his mother bore

Him, with what (if any) handicaps at birth;
did he wish free enterprise to thrive;
what precisely was he up to on this earth,

What were his beliefs and total worth.
Noncompliance might result in in-
stant imprisonment. Signed: Ralph T. Lynne.

Korf replies: Let Undersigned be thought
by the High Initiating Force
a Congenitally disembodied Naught

qua Material Resource, although of course
Livened by Ineffable Regret—as must
be the more robust Official Source.

Ralph T. Lynne peruses this nonplussed.

Die Behörde

Korf erhält vom Polizeibüro
ein geharnischt Formular,
wer er sei und wie und wo.

Welchen Orts er bis anheute war,
welchen Stands und überhaupt,
wo geboren, Tag und Jahr.

Ob ihm überhaupt erlaubt,
hier zu leben und zu welchem Zweck,

wieviel Geld er hat und was er glaubt
Umgekehrten Falls man ihn vom Fleck

in Arrest verführen würde, und
drunter steht: Borowsky, Heck.

Korf erwidert darauf kurz und rund:

,Einer hohen Direktion
stellt sich, laut persönlichem Befund,

untig angefertigte Person
als nichtexistent im Eigen-Sinn
bürgerlicher Konvention

vor und aus, und zeichnet
wennschonhin mitbedauernd, Korf.'
Staunend liest's der anbetroffne Chef.

Korf's reply delivers a fine spray of sarcasm by which an apolo-
getic nonentity, sure of baffling the bovine bureaucracy, foils
questionnaires; very like the tactics of the brave soldier Švejk.

Metaphor

Palmström teeters like a windblown twig . . .
Asked by Korf why he is thus adrift
He explains: an exquisite conceit,
Like a bird alighting, soft and fleet,
Had but touched him with its parting lift—
So he teetered like a windblown twig,
Swaying still with the delightful gift.

Gleichnis

Palmström schwankt als wie ein Zweig im Wind . . .
Als ihn Korf befragt, warum er schwanke,
meint er: weil ein lieblicher Gedanke,
wie ein Vogel, zärtlich und geschwind,
auf ein kleines ihn belastet habe—
schwanke er als wie ein Zweig im Wind,
schwingend noch von der willkommnen Gabe . . .

Two Parties

Korf and Palmström each arrange a feast.

Palmström has the whole world gathering
Just to fast—sole purpose of the fling!
Just one day to gorge on not a thing!
Yield: a fund to aid the starved and fleeced.

Korf for his part goes among the stricken
By disease, by need, by spite, alas,
And attempts to move their feelings so
That this day they turn from hate or wrath,
That within their souls they come to know
Pity wide enough for all the "wicked."

In a word, both offer people *giving*,
Not indulging, in the hope that, after all,
Men who think instead of merely living
Need such parties to rejoice at all.

Die beiden Feste

Korf und Palmström geben je ein Fest.

Dieser lädt die ganze Welt zu Gaste:
doch allein zum Zwecke, daß sie—faste!
einen Tag lang sich mit nichts belaste!
Und ein—Antihungersnotfonds ist der Rest.

Korf hingegen wandert zu den Armen,
zu den Krüppeln und den leider Schlimmen
und versucht sie alle so zu stimmen,
daß sie einen Tag lang nicht ergrimmen,
daß in ihnen anhebt aufzuglimmen
ein jedweden ‚Feind‘ umfassendes—Erbarmen.

Beide lassen so die Menschen schenken
statt genießen, und sie meinen: freuen

könnten Wesen (die nun einmal—denken)

sich allein an solchen gänzlich neuen Festen.

————

Part Three

Palma
Kunkel

Palma Kunkel

Palma Kunkel is akin to Palm,
For the rest, however, an unknown.
And the fact occasions her no qualm;
She prefers to live quite on her own.

Thus the scribe remains completely mute
On Miss Kunkel's nature and pursuit.
Only when she issues from the dark
Does he duly enter a remark.

But he finds no issue to report,
Nor the least intention of the sort.
Even that her name was bruited here
Is a crass invasion of her sphere.

Palma Kunkel

Palma Kunkel ist mit Palm verwandt,
doch im übrigen sonst nicht bekannt.
Und sie wünscht auch nicht bekannt zu sein,
lebt am liebsten ganz für sich allein.

Über Muhme Palma Kunkel drum
bleibt auch der Chronist vollkommen stumm.
Nur wo selbst sie aus dem Dunkel tritt,
teilt er dies ihr Treten treulich mit.

Doch sie trat bis jetzt noch nicht ans Licht,
und sie will es auch in Zukunft nicht.
Schon, dass hier ihr Name lautbar ward,
widerspricht vollkommen ihrer Art.

———

The Book Label

An anonymus from Tibris
Sends to Palma an Ex libris.

This shows nothing but the white
Luster of unsullied light,

By no faintest imprint grooved.
Palma feels profoundly moved;

All her books the gift enables
Her to mark with virgin labels.

Exlibris

Ein Anonymus aus Tibris
sendet Palman ein Exlibris.

Auf demselben sieht man nichts
als den weißen Schein des Lichts.

Nicht ein Strichlein ist vorhanden.
Palma fühlt sich warm verstanden.

Und sie klebt die Blättlein rein
allenthalben dankbar ein.

———

Saving Breath

Oh yes, Palma talks, I'll have you know.
Not like children of the darkness, though.

Not awash in tumbling words, like most:
Ever meditating pre-, not post-.

Alien quite to reckless, feckless sounds,
She will question but on solid grounds.

Ask the dumbard never, just the wiz-,
Nor the latter merely how he is.

Won't discuss the weather or the roast,
But their ontic essences at most.

Thus she stays unspent and sound as oak,
For her breath is not dispersed like smoke.

Wort-Kunst

Palma Kunkel spricht auch. O gewiß.
Freilich nicht wie Volk der Finsternis.

Nicht von Worten kollernd wie ein Bronnen,
niemals nachwärts-, immer vorbesonnen.

Völlig fremd den hilflos vielen Schällen,
fragt sie nur in wirklich großen Fällen.

Fragt den Zwergen niemals, nur den Riesen,
und auch nicht, wie es ihm gehe, diesen.

Nicht vom Wetter spricht sie, nicht vom Schneider,
höchstens von den Grundproblemen beider.

Und so bleibt sie jung und unverbraucht,
weil ihr Odem nicht wie Dunst verraucht.

Deer Mail

Miss Kunkel vacations where no one intrudes;
At a gamekeeper's cottage in Neck-of-the-Woods,

Where the mailing of letters is carried out
By a warden or logger (whoever's about)

Just hanging them up on the antlers or tails
Of the bucks on the neighboring wildlife trails;

Then, at the close of the hunting season,
They're forwarded—late, but not out of reason.

Both the game and the neighbors are proud of the post;
And never one letter has ever been lost.

Das Forsthaus

Palma Kunkel ist häufig zum Kuraufenthalt
in einem einsamen Forsthaus weit hinten im Wald,
von wo ein Brief so befördert wird,
daß ihn, wer gerade Zeit hat, ein Knecht oder Hirt
dem Wild des angrenzenden Jagdrevieres
um Hals oder Bein hängt . . . worauf in des Tieres
erfolgender Schußzeit er, wenn auch oft spät,
auf ein Postamt und von dort an seine Adresse gerät.
So das Wild wie die Nachbarn sind stolz auf die Ehre,
Und man weiß keinen Fall, daß ein Brief je verloren
    gegangen wäre.

————————

The Parrot

Palma's parrot scorns applause,
Unlike extroverted birds;
Never, for whatever cause,
Has he yet pronounced his words.

And their number's numberless,
For he is the wisest fowl
Ever sold, from awk to owl,
Breeding's most august success.

Yet his tongue seems tied as he
Scans you with a frigid stare,
And whoever you may be,
Not a whisper will he share.

Der Papagei

Palma Kunkels Papagei
spekuliert nicht auf Applaus;
niemals, was auch immer sei,
spricht er seine Wörter aus.

Deren Zahl ist ohne Zahl:
denn er ist das klügste Tier,
das man je zum Kauf empfahl,
und der Zucht vollkommne Zier.

Doch indem er streng dich mißt,
scheint sein Zungenglied verdorrt.
Gleichviel, wer du immer bist,
er verrät dir nicht ein Wort.

"Polly"

What is the parrot's name? someone will ask.
But no one will let no one lift its mask.

Just once it found itself addressed as "Polly,"
And fell for many weeks in melancholy.

It only grew completely whole and sound
Through a new friend—Fritz Kunkel's youthful hound.

‚Lore'

Wie heißt der Papagei? wird mancher fragen.
Doch nie wird jemand jemandem dies sagen.

Er ward einmal mit ‚Lore' angesprochen—
und fiel darauf in Wehmut viele Wochen.

Er ward erst wieder voll und ganz gesund
durch einen Freund: Fritz Kunkels jungen Hund.

————

Pollo

Fritz Kunkel's hound was bought, a nameless orph,
By a stepfosterbrother of von Korf.

The moment he, unselfish to a fault,
Learnt of the onomastical assault,

He sought the bird and, nameless as he was,
Espoused the name of "Pollo" in its cause:

Whereby the parrot, as it were, was freed,
And all the world abashed by this pure deed!

Von Korf performed the christening himself;
And the poor bird at once regained its health.

Lorus

Fritz Kunkels Pudel ward, noch ungetauft,
von einem Stiefmilchbruder Korfs gekauft.

Es trieb ihn, als er, hilfreich von Natur,
der sogenannten ,Lore' Leid erfuhr,

sogleich zu ihr: worauf er, der nicht hieß,
sich ihr zum Troste Lorus taufen ließ:

den Namen also gleichsam auf sich nehmend—
und alle Welt durch diese Tat beschämend!

Korf selbst vollzog den Taufakt unverweilt.
Der Vogel aber war fortan geheilt.

———

The Tomcat

Pollo, in exploring his new sphere,
Meets the first tomcat of his career,

Whom the ancient reflex of his troupe,
Loops into an instant fearsome hoop.

Pollo, though, undaunted young Franciscan,
Chants: Dear fellow creature, pax vobiscum!

Der Kater

Lorus, im Verlaufe seines Strebens,
trifft den ersten Kater seines Lebens.

Dieser krümmt, traditionellerweis,
seinen Rücken fürchterlich zum Kreis.

Lorus spricht mit unerschrockner Zärte:
‚Pax vobiscum, freundlicher Gefährte!'

Anyone taken aback by the last rhyme may take solace from
the first rhyme of the preceding poem, yet to be extirpated.

Peke's Peak

Most lapdogs like to loll on padded seats
In windows that project above the streets,

In order from this snug and lofty sill
To watch the motley world revolve and mill.

O man! Eschew this habit if you will,
Lest you be but a pug upon a sill.

Mopsenleben

Es sitzen Möpse gern auf Mauerecken,
die sich ins Straßenbild hinaus erstrecken,

um von sotanen vorteilhaften Posten
die bunte Welt gemächlich auszukosten.

O Mensch, lieg vor dir selber auf der Lauer,
sonst bist du auch ein Mops nur auf der Mauer.

———

84

The Milestone

Deep in forest gloom it hides,
And upon its front is carved,
Lest the wanderer's mind be starved:
Fourteen miles to Riversides.

Strange to think, in fact unnerving:
There's no text, unless a seeing
Eye is present to be serving
As the agent of its being.

Further be the thought unfurled:
What is there without such action?
Why, a fathomless abstraction!
Eye alone creates the world.

Der Meilenstein

Tief im dunklen Walde steht er
und auf ihm mit schwarzer Farbe,
daß des Wandrers Geist nicht darbe:
Dreiundzwanzig Kilometer.

Seltsam ist und schier zum Lachen,
daß es diesen Text nicht gibt,
wenn es keinem Blick beliebt,
ihn durch sich zu Text zu machen.

Und noch weiter vorgestellt:
Was wohl ist er—ungesehen?
Ein uns völlig fremd Geschehen.
Erst das Auge schafft die Welt.

In a philosophy tutorial at Oxford the above problem took the
form of a dialogue in limericks, approximately as follows:

There was a young man who said "God
must find it exceedingly odd
   if he sees that this tree
   continues to be
when there's no one about in the quad."

"Dear Sir, your bemusement is odd:
I am always about in the quad:
   and that's how this tree
   continues to be
Observed by
           Yours faithfully
                God."

———————

Telescopy

A rabbit sat upon a pleasance,
Assured of no extraneous presence.

But from an upland at some distance
A man possessed of calm persistence,

His spyglass trained upon that mead
Is watching little long-ears feed.

At him in turn, from far uphill,
A god is gazing, mild and still.

Vice Versa

Ein Hase sitzt auf einer Wiese,
des Glaubens, niemand sähe diese.

Doch, im Besitze eines Zeißes,
betrachtet voll gehaltnen Fleißes

vom vis-à-vis gelegnen Berg
ein Mensch den kleinen Löffelzwerg.

Ihn aber blickt hinwiederum
ein Gott von fern an, mild und stumm.

The Unicorn

The unicorn, that erstwhile hub
Of quests, survives but as a pub.

One visits it at eve, if male,
And hooks one's foot around the rail.

Some centuries from now, who knows,
We too may figure, I suppose,

Irrevocably sublimated,
As mere hotels where guests are sated,

And lolling in the "Man and Child,"
They'll sip their pints of mild.

Das Einhorn

Das Einhorn lebt von Ort zu Ort
nur noch als Wirtshaus fort.

Man geht hinein zur Abendstund
und sitzt den Stammtisch rund.

Wer weiß! Nach Jahr und Tag sind wir
auch ganz wie jenes Tier

Hotels nur noch, darin man speist—
(so völlig wurden wir zu Geist).

Im ‚Goldnen Menschen' sitzt man dann
und sagt sein Solo an . . .

This is one of several poems showing Morgenstern's inclination
to redress the moral balance between man and beast.

———

The Lox

A lox swam up the Rhine
beyond the Ruhr and Main.

He rode the upper flow
past fifty falls or so.

But then he had to clear
a Swiss design of weir

he had not met before—
two fathoms high or more!

Ten feet he smartly scaled—
but here his courage failed.

Three weeks he faced the wall
behind the waterfall,

then swam, not saying much,
back to the French and Dutch.

Der Salm

Ein Rheinsalm schwamm den Rhein
bis in die Schweiz hinein.

Und sprang den Oberlauf
von Fall zu Fall hinauf.

Er war schon weißgottwo,
doch eines Tages—oh!—

da kam er an ein Wehr:
das maß zwölf Fuß und mehr!

Zehn Fuß—die sprang er gut!
Doch hier zerbrach sein Mut.

Drei Wochen stand der Salm
am Fuß der Wasser-Alm.

Und kehrte schließlich stumm
nach Deutsch- und Holland um.

———————

The Raven

A brook named Raven, as it crawls
'twixt foggy banks at night, recalls
amidst this clammy business
the erstwhile metamorphosis
which these one thousand years ago
a wizard made it undergo.

And as the fogbanks swathe and brew,
its former selfhood wakes anew.
It boards the body of a crow
that chanced to sleep nearby, and so
takes wing (its brook-bed left to parch)
and flies away through pine and larch.

Die Elster

Ein Bach, mit Namen Elster, rinnt
durch Nacht und Nebel und besinnt
inmitten dieser stillen Handlung
sich seiner einstigen Verwandlung,
die ihm vor mehr als tausend Jahren
von einem Magier widerfahren.

Und wie so Nacht und Nebel weben,
erwacht in ihm das alte Leben.
Er fährt in eine in der Nähe
zufällig eingeschlafne Krähe
und fliegt, dieweil sein Bett verdorrt,
wie dermaleinst als Vogel fort.

———

Enquiry about the Foregoing

The ichthyologist Bruce Bowing
inclines to credit the foregoing.
Old Ovid told this sort of thing;
but one point has him wondering:

"What," he enquires, somewhat torn,
"about the fish-world of that bourn?
Does it turn bird, too, or instead
stay in the brook-bed, left for dead?"

Himself, he would have opted for
the former, but the latter bore
more likelihood: when first we heard
that such a wonder once occurred,

the Pica had been, this we know,
translated by the mighty foe
into a stream that, first conceived
as fishless, only then received

from tributary creeks in part,
in part by means of human art,
a stock of piscine population
for customary habitation.

To ascertain the fishes' fate,
it would be most appropriate
to probe the brook-bed to the ground,
however toilsome it was found.

Anfrage

Der Ichthyologe Berthold Schrauben
will Umiges dem Autor glauben.
Er kennt dergleichen aus Oviden,
doch Eines raubt ihm seinen Frieden:

‚Wo nämlich‘, fragt er, ‚bleibt die Stelle
der Fischwelt obbenannter Quelle?
Verkörpert sie sich mit zum Raben—
oder verbleibt sie tot im Graben?‘

Persönlich sei er für das erste,
dem zweiten aber sei die mehrste
Wahrscheinlichkeit zu geben, da,
als seinerzeit die Tat geschah,

die Pica von dem mächtigen Feinde
in einen ohne Fischgemeinde
zunächst gedachten Wasserlauf
verwandelt worden sei, worauf

erst später jene, teils durch Neben-
gewässer, teils durch Menschenstreben,
als übliche Bewohnersphäre
ihm eingegliedert worden wäre.

Es sei für einen Fall wie diesen
von Nennwert, nicht unangewiesen,
wenn er, empfänd mans gleich als Bürde,
bis auf den Grund durchleuchtet würde.

The Sandwich Bag, or Spontaneous Gestation Blighted

A sandwich bag among some trees,
When snowed upon, began to freeze.
In its alarm, while not the brightest,
And never having had the slightest
Forethought of thinking (nor it ought,
Composed of rags and such) bethought
(From terror, mind) itself to think,
Began, set out, commenced to think,
(Imagine, if you please, the strain!),
Evolved (from fear, I said) a brain . . .
And not, I scarcely need to mention,
By vague celestial intervention,
But with a quite (in panic's vortex)
Correctly formed anterior cortex,
Which from albumen, starch and stuff
(Through fear) with overleaping of
The customary eons found
In it Gestalt and living ground
[(with overleaping) in and through
It living-ground and structure grew)].

Assisted by this helpful fact,
The sandwich bag began to act,
To—live, to—well, I hardly know,
It moved an insect step or so,
Began to crawl and then to fly,
Soared from the undergrowth and high
Across the roadway, fro and yon
And hither and athwart and on—
However such a thing reacts
To world and wind (and other facts).

But friends! Stand by me in my need!
A bird, obese and full of greed,
Espies it (this is wintertide)
And makes as if with hair and hide . . .
And makes as if with root and branch . . .

(Who dares go on with this?) (I blanch)—
(Consider, will you, what it took!)—
And starts, with sinker, line and hook . . .
A sandwich bag in strain and strife
Attains . . . through fear . . . organic life . . .
Enough! The savage at one gulp
Devours the priceless bit of pulp.

Das Butterbrotpapier

Ein Butterbrotpapier im Wald,—
da es beschneit wird, fühlt sich kalt . . .

In seiner Angst, wiewohl es nie
an Denken vorher irgendwie

gedacht, natürlich, als ein Ding
aus Lumpen usw., fing,

aus Angst, so sagte ich, fing an
zu denken, fing, hob an, begann,

zu denken, denkt euch, was das heißt,
bekam (aus Angst, so sagt' ich)—Geist,

und zwar, versteht sich, nicht bloß so
vom Himmel droben irgendwo,

vielmehr infolge einer ganz
exakt entstandnen Hirnsubstanz—

die aus Holz, Eiweiß, Mehl und Schmer,
(durch Angst,) mit Überspringung der

sonst üblichen Weltalter, an
ihm Boden und Gefäß gewann—

[(mit Überspringung) in und an
ihm Boden und Gefäß gewann].

Mit Hilfe dieser Hilfe nun
entschloß sich das Papier zum Tun,—

zum Leben, zum—gleichviel, es fing
zu gehn an—wie ein Schmetterling . . .

zu kriechen erst, zu fliegen drauf,
bis übers Unterholz hinauf,

dann über die Chaussee und quer
und kreuz und links und hin und her—

wie eben solch ein Tier zur Welt
(je nach dem Wind) (und sonst) sich stellt.

Doch, Freunde! werdet bleich gleich mir!—:
Ein Vogel, dick und ganz voll Gier,

erblickts (wir sind im Januar . . .)—
und schickt sich an, mit Haut und Haar—

und schickt sich an, mit Haar und Haut—
(wer mag da endigen!) (mir graut)—

(Bedenkt, was alles nötig war!)—
und schickt sich an, mit Haut und Haar—

Ein Butterbrotpapier im Wald
gewinnt—aus Angst—Naturgestalt . . .

Genug!! Der wilde Specht verschluckt
das unersetzliche Produkt . . .

———

The Mouse-Eye

The red eye of a mouse
Peers from its mousehole house.

It sets the dusk aglitter.
The heart goes patter-pitter.

"The heart of whom?" The heart of me!
I sit before the mouse, you see.

Reflect upon this mouse, for oh!
All is awesome here below.

Das Auge der Maus

Das rote Auge einer Maus
lugt aus dem Loch heraus.

Es funkelt durch die Dämmerung . . .
Das Herz gerät in Hämmerung.

‚Das Herz von wem?' Das Herz von mir!
Ich sitze nämlich vor dem Tier.

Oh, Seele, denk an diese Maus!
Alle Dinge sind voll Graus.

———

Fate

The storm-cloud's zigzag zonker bright
Cried "I bring you, my mutton, light!"

The ram, who had not left his barn,
Was singed amidships and astarn.

He has been brooding ever since
Oh why this fell on him, and whence.

Schicksal

Der Wolke Zickzackzunge spricht:
ich bringe dir, mein Hammel, Licht.

Der Hammel, der im Stalle stand,
ward links und hinten schwarz gebrannt.

Sein Leben grübelt er seitdem:
warum ihm dies geschah von wem?

————

The Sparrow and the Kangaroo
Behind its fence the kangaroo—
It squats, a sparrow in its view.

The sparrow perches on its tree
With slowly waning gaiety.

It feels as it is crouching there
The kangaroo's persistent stare.

The sparrow shakes its ruff of feather—
This is too eery altogether.

It feels increasingly unseated . . .
What if the kangaroo should eat it?!

Whereas the kangaroo instead
An hour from this inclines its head

With or without profound reflection
Into a different direction.

Der Sperling und das Känguruh
In seinem Zaun das Känguruh—
es hockt und guckt dem Sperling zu.

Der Sperling sitzt auf dem Gebäude—
doch ohne sonderliche Freude.

Vielmehr, er fühlt, den Kopf geduckt,
wie ihn das Känguruh beguckt.

Der Sperling sträubt den Federflaus—
die Sache ist auch gar zu kraus.

Ihm ist, als ob er kaum noch säße . . .
Wenn nun das Känguruh ihn fräße?!

Doch dieses dreht nach einer Stunde
den Kopf aus irgend einem Grunde,

vielleicht auch ohne tiefern Sinn,
nach einer andern Richtung hin.

————

The Canceled Buck

As extra in a royal cast,
A roebuck had the nightly task
In Act Two, at the cry of "hounds!"
To burst onstage with fearful bounds.

The thirteenth time, he missed the stage
And crashed into the prompter's cage;
So promptly both his part and he
Were dropped from play and company.

Two liveried retainers came
At dawn to drive the cashiered game,
No longer qualified to serve,
Back to the royal deer preserve.

Where now the venison feels called
To hold its audience enthralled—
Wild boar and beaver, fox and shrew—
With "star part," "center stage," and "cue."

Der gestrichene Bock

Ein Wildbret mußt allabendlich
auf einem Hoftheater sich
im Hauptakt auf das Stichwort ‚Schürzen'
von links aus der Kulisse stürzen.

Beim zwölften Male brach es aus
und rannte dem Souffleur ins Haus,
worauf es kurzweg—und sein Part—
von der Regie gestrichen ward.

Zwei Hoftheaterdiener brachten
am nächsten Morgen den gedachten
gestrichnen königlichen Bock
per Auto nach Hubertusstock.

Dort geht das Wildbret nun herum
und unterhält sein Publikum
aus Reh, Hirsch, Eber, Fuchs und Maus
von ,Rolle', ,Stichwort' und ,Applaus'.

———

Parable

Two porkers, with a hen between,
Reposed amid a rustic scene.

The hen, as one is apt to find
(In proverbs, anyway), was blind.

The swine were simply swine, you see,
Of utmost authenticity.

These three a man took unawares.
(A woman, possibly; who cares?)

He stepped across and gave the shoats—
You are expecting beets or oats?

Wrong! Pearls he was observed to scatter,
And guineas (she, then! Does it matter?).

The porkers dropped their lids, inert.
The hen, though, modest but alert,

Arose with neither haste nor scorn
And ate the gems like so much corn.

The man slunk off in clouded spirits;
But the Almighty weighed the merits

Of those three parties and decreed
That to this faithful chicken's seed

External jewels be awarded.
Whereby this Planet was afforded

The guinea pig? Don't be facetious!
The guinea *hen*—a bright new species.

Tertium Gaudens
(Ein Stück Entwicklungsgeschichte)

Zwei Säue taten um ein Huhn
In einem Korb zusammenruhn.

Das Huhn, wie Hühner manchmal sind
(Im Sprichwort mindestens), war blind.

Die Säue waren schlechtweg Säue,
Von völliger Naturgetreue.

Dies Dreieck nahm ein Mann zum Ziel.
Vielleicht wars auch ein Weib, gleichviel.

Er trat heran und gab den Schweinen—
Ihr werdet Runkelrüben meinen.

O nein: er warf (er oder sie)
Warf Perlen vor das schnöde Vieh!

Die Säue schlossen träg die Lider.
Das Huhn indessen, still und bieder,

Erhob sich sonder Hast und Zorn
Und frass die Perlen auf wie Korn.

Der Mensch entwich und sann auf Rache.
Doch Gott im Himmel wog die Sache

Der drei Parteien und entschied,
Dass dieses Huhn im nächsten Glied

Die Perlen *aussen* tragen solle.
Wodurch die alte Erdenscholle

Das Perlschwein? Nein—das war verspielt!
Das Perl*huhn* zum Geschenk erhielt.

———

The Jagua

A tear-off calendar of Nicaragua
Displays the frontal likeness of a jagua.

It looks at you, intent and sober,
Throughout the nineteenth of October.

Whereby it ventures to recall
That it is extant, after all.

Der Leu

Auf einem Wandkalenderblatt
ein Leu sich abgebildet hat.

Er blickt dich an, bewegt und still,
den ganzen 17. April.

Wodurch er zu erinnern liebt,
daß es ihn immerhin noch gibt.

As elsewhere in this collection, the translator has seen fit to re-
place inconvenient names and places by equivalent handier
ones—without loss of local color; here he has changed felines.

———

The Birth of Philosophy
The moorland mutton stares at me in awe,
As if I were the first of men it saw.
Its gaze infects; we stand as if asleep;
This seems the first time I have seen a sheep.

Geburtsakt der Philosophie
Erschrocken staunt der Heide Schaf mich an,
als säh's in mir den ersten Menschenmann.
Sein Blick steckt an; wir stehen wie im Schlaf;
mir ist, ich säh' zum ersten Mal ein Schaf.

———

The Two Parallels

Two parallels departed,
On the nonfinite bent,
Two souls of simplehearted
Inflexible intent.

There'd be no intersecting
In this world or the next,
The two had vowed, reflecting
Their inmost creed and text.

Ten light-years, sternly double,
They wandered side by side;
At last the lonesome couple
Grew strange to earthly pride.

Were they still parallels?
They hardly knew themselves;
They coursed through dazzling spells
Like two ethereal elves.

God's changeless light enorbed them,
And they grew one in him;
Eternity absorbed them,
A pair of seraphim.

Die zwei Parallelen

Es gingen zwei Parallelen
ins Endlose hinaus,
zwei kerzengerade Seelen
und aus solidem Haus.

Sie wollten sich nicht schneiden
bis an ihr seliges Grab:
Das war nun einmal der beiden
geheimer Stolz und Stab.

Doch als sie zehn Lichtjahre
gewandert neben sich hin,
da ward's dem einsamen Paare
nicht irdisch mehr zu Sinn.

War'n sie noch Parallelen?
Sie wußten's selber nicht,—
sie flossen nur wie zwei Seelen
zusammen durch ewiges Licht.

Das ewige Licht durchdrang sie,
da wurden sie eins in ihm;
die Ewigkeit verschlang sie
als wie zwei Seraphim.

———

Memorial

Make my monument, chéri,
All of sugar, deep at sea.

A sweetwater lake will rise
(Briefly, true) from my demise.

Long enough, though, for a hundred
Fishes to have sipped and wondered.

Then, at Bremen, say, these mullets
Are consumed by human gullets.

Thus with natural decorum
I rejoin your pleasant forum,

While, if bronze I turn or stone,
Birds their stern ends, let alone

Men of worth their persiflage
At my personage discharge.

Denkmalswunsch

Setze mir ein Denkmal, cher,
ganz aus Zucker, tief im Meer.

Ein Süßwassersee, zwar kurz,
werd ich dann nach meinem Sturz;

doch so lang, daß Fische, hundert,
nehmen einen Schluck verwundert.—
Diese ißt in Hamburg und
Bremen dann des Menschen Mund.—

Wiederum in eure Kreise
komm ich so auf gute Weise,

während, werd ich Stein und Erz,
nur ein Vogel seinen Sterz

oder gar ein Mensch von Wert
seinen Witz auf mich entleert.

The translator has overcome his serious doubts about mullets
in the North Sea.

————

Part Four

Lost
in
Thought

The Esthete

I would rather when I sit
Not sit as my sitting flesh,
But as my esprit-de-siège
If it sat, would braid its seat.

It has few demands or rules,
Values only styles in stools,
Leaves their purpose envy-free
To the mob's rapacity.

Der Aesthet

Wenn ich sitze, will ich nicht
sitzen, wie mein Sitz-Fleisch möchte,
sondern wie mein Sitz-Geist sich,
säße er, den Stuhl sich flöchte.

Der jedoch bedarf nicht viel,
schätzt am Stuhl allein den Stil,
überläßt den Zweck des Möbels
ohne Grimm der Gier des Pöbels.

———

St. Oopsadaise
Secluded in his island maze
resides the sacred Oopsadaise.

You're silent? Have they taped you up?
You doubt that he exists, young pup?

Then let me volunteer this, sport:
He does exist, like it or not;

St. Oopsadaise of pious fame,
And he's the third to bear the name.

He prays for you, you little pest,
Because you sin, like all the rest.

You don't know what you owe to him—
you're back from fire or climb, or swim

as neither floater, stiff, or cinder?
You owe it to this stout defender

from sundry ills of life. Oh hell—
The world is round and man is frail.

Der heilige Pardauz
Im Inselwald ‚Zum stillen Kauz‘,
da lebt der heilige Pardauz.

Du schweigst? Ist dir der Mund verklebt?
Du zweifelst, ob er wirklich lebt?

So sag ich's dir denn ungefragt:
Er lebt, auch wenn dir's mißbehagt.

Er lebt im Wald, ‚Zum stillen Kauz‘,
und schon sein Vater hieß Pardauz.

Dort betet er für dich, mein Kind,
weil du und andre Sünder sind.

Du weißt nicht, was du ihm verdankst,—
doch daß du nicht schon längst ertrankst,

verbranntest oder und so weiter—
das dankst du diesem Blitzableiter

der teuflischen Gewitter. Ach,
die Welt ist rund, der Mensch ist schwach.

German *Pardauz!* is a nursery noise celebrating a simple or
complex leap, especially when unsuccessful. The testy tone of
the poem clearly forestalls the reader's offensive skepticism.

———

Inshallah and Mashallah

Insh- and Mashallah are twin
magickers from Bab-el-Jinn,

Sworn by Zri, the mighty Zra,
To my service from afar.

If I lack—whatever thing,
like a tree, a proof, a ring,

I call Insh-, and he, transvested,
turns into the thing requested;

Whereas Mashallah instead,
enters what one likes to shed.

Say you have an itchy rash—
Rash will promptly change to Mash-;

Were you felled by murder, say,
Death, as Mash-, will go away.

Truly Insh- and Mash- ensure
days serene and nights secure.

Let all follow, then, the star
of said Zri, the mighty Zra.

Golch und Flubis

Golch und Flubis, das sind zwei
Gaukler aus der Titanei,

die mir einst in einer Nacht
Zri, die große Zra, vermacht.

Mangelt irgend mir ein Ding,
ein Beweis, ein Baum, ein Ring—

ruf ich Golch, und er verwandelt
sich in das, worum sichs handelt.

Während Flubis umgekehrt
das wird, was man gern entbehrt.

Bei z. B. Halsbeschwerden
wird das Halsweh Flubis werden.

Fällte dich z. B. Mord,
ging der Tod als Flubis fort.

Lieblich lebt es sich mit solchen
wackern Flubissen und Golchen.

Darum suche jeder ja
dito Zri, die große Zra.

————

The Sniffle

A sniffle lurks by the terrace stair;
It hopes to catch a victim there.

And presently, with talons grim,
It pounces on a man named Schrimm.

Paul Schrimm kerchoos to rock a rafter
And "has" it till the Monday after.

Der Schnupfen

Ein Schnupfen hockt auf der Terrasse,
auf dass er sich ein Opfer fasse

—und stürzt alsbald mit grossem Grimm
auf einen Menschen namens Schrimm.

Paul Schrimm erwidert prompt: ‚Pitschü!'
und ‚hat' ihn drauf bis Montag früh.

———

Kitchen Debate

A half-a-tbs. and a full tsp.
Had words together, proud and crsp.

The tsp. said: "I am more than you!"
The half-a-tbs. called this untrue.

Till Science, putting both to shame,
Held kitchen language up to blame.

"You are," it ruled effectively,
"Five and ten grams, respectively."

Etiketten-Frage

Ein halfer Eßl. und ein Teel.
besahn einander stolz und scheel.

Der Teel. erklärte: ‚Ich bin mehr!'
Der halbe Eßl. rief, nein, er!

Die Wissenschaft entschied voll Hohn:
Das kommt vom populären Ton.

‚Ihr seid', sprach patzig die Madam,
‚einfach fünf Gramm und zehen Gramm.'

Strictly Punctuation

The realm of punctuation groans
With civil factions all at odds:

The semicols. are labeled drones
By commas and by periods.

These promptly found a league they dub
The Anti-Semicolon Club.

Alone to fade into the hallways
Are the moot question marks (as always).

The semicols., in dire unease,
Are cornered in parentheses,

And isolated thus, at leisure
Clamped into brackets for good measure.

The minus sign now joins the strife
And snip! deducts them all from life.

The question marks, returning, look
Bemused upon the donnybrook.

But woe! A fresh contention gapes:
The dashes jump the comma shapes—

As lances they bisect their crops
Until they too, all hooks and stops,

(This by the formers' fell designs)
Succumb as semicolon signs! . . .

To funeral pyres are consigned
The semicols. of either kind.

What of the dashes is still here
Limps black and tacit in the rear.

The exclamation point is urged
With colon-boys to bless the ash;

Then, of all curlicuing purged,
They lumber home, dot, dash, dot, dash . . .

Im Reich der Interpunktionen

Im Reich der Interpunktionen
nicht fürder goldener Friede prunkt:

Die Semikolons werden Drohnen
genannt von Beistrich und von Punkt.

Es bildet sich zur selben Stund
ein Antisemikolonbund.

Die einzigen, die stumm entweichen
(wie immer), sind die Fragezeichen.

Die Semikolons, die sehr jammern,
umstellt man mit geschwungnen Klammern

und setzt die so gefangnen Wesen
noch obendrein in Parenthesen.

Das Minuszeichen naht, und—schwapp!
da zieht es sie vom Leben ab.

Kopfschüttelnd blicken auf die Leichen
die heimgekehrten Fragezeichen.

Doch, wehe! neuer Kampf sich schürzt:
Gedankenstrich auf Komma stürzt—

und fährt ihm schneidend durch den Hals,
bis dieser gleich—und ebenfalls

(wie jener mörderisch bezweckt)
als Strichpunkt das Gefild bedeckt! . . .

Stumm trägt man auf den Totengarten
die Semikolons beider Arten.

Was übrig von Gedankenstrichen,
Kommt schwarz und schweigsam nachgeschlichen.

Das Ausrufzeichen hält die Predigt;
das Kolon dient ihm als Adjunkt.

Dann, jeder Kommaform entledigt,
Stapft heimwärts man, Strich, Punkt, Strich, Punkt . . .

––––––––

The Camelepard

The camelepard roams the wold
In search of keeper Heribold.

The while the keeper for his part
pursues it with the woodsman's art

And poisoned musketballs designed
To turn to smoke the thing they find.

They coincide at last, and pop!
He shoots it, and it eats him up.

The venom, though, still wreaks its doom!
Both game and contents turn to fume.

They flourish now as leitmotifs
Of migrant popular beliefs.

Das Löwenreh

Das Löwenreh durcheilt den Wald
und sucht den Förster Theobald.

Der Förster Theobald desgleichen
sucht es durch Pirschen zu erreichen,

und zwar mit Kugeln, deren Gift
zu Rauch verwandelt, wen es trifft.

Als sie sich endlich haben, schießt
er es, worauf es ihn genießt.

Allein die Kugel wirkt alsbald:
Zu Rauch wird Reh nebst Theobald . . .

Seitdem sind beide ohne Frage
ein dankbares Objekt der Sage.

The camelepard, like the more notorious unicorn, was a crea-
ture of medieval fancy, not Morgenstern's. He turns it into a
"lion deer," shaggy on top and svelte behind, a blond buffalo
calf or young Oscar Wilde may help us visualize it. The magic
bullets, of course, create a unique situation.

———————

Letter from Mrs. Davy Jones

My wedded lord, dear Skull-and-bones,
Horribeloved Davy Jones!
I thank you kindly for your note
And for staying four more weeks on the boat.

The *Marfa*'s a well-found ship, God bless;
But remember the crags of Devil's Ness.
I live here calmly as before;
Things have been quiet around the Nore.

Sometimes I stop for five-o'clock tea
At an elf-light's in the vicinity;
She is uncommon obliging and pretty,
But speaks only Lettish, more's the pity.

1-6-04, by St. Marylebone's.
Your devoted wife, Mistress Martha Jones.

Brief einer Klabauterfrau

Mein lieber und vertrauter Mann,
entsetzlieber Klabautermann,
ich danke dir, für was du schreibst
und daß du noch vier Wochen bleibst.

Die ‚Marfa' ist ein schönes Schiff,
vergiß nur nicht das Teufelsriff;
ich lebe hier ganz unnervos,
denn auf der Elbe ist nichts los.

Bei einem Irrlicht in der Näh
trink manchmal ich den Fünfuhrtee,
doch weil sie leider Böhmisch spricht,
verstehen wir einander nicht.

1. 6. 04. Stadt Trautenau.

Deine getreue Klabauterfrau.

The Klabautermann, who haunted German sailors as Davy
Jones did English ones, was not known to have a wife before
Morgenstern discovered this letter.

———————

Little Legends of the Devil

(1) The Painter

A painter, high up in a church,
Lampooned amid his fresco's jungle
The Devil like a slavering mongrel:
Who promptly pushed him off his perch.

But lower down the Virgin stood;
She stretched her hand to break his fall
And offered for a pedestal
The tiptoe of her tiny foot.

And whispered to his ashen face:
"Thus your Young Lady pays the score
To scamps who boast—but who before
Portrayed her with such charm and grace!"

(2) The Rabbi

A rabbi of Prague, in league with the Devil,
To such strong magic did attain
That dreaded Death himself would level
His glittering scythe at him in vain.

Yet Death in the end did lay him low:
He hid in a rose's perfumed tent.
The fiend hadn't though of the rose, and so
The Rabbi died of the rose's scent.

I. Der Maler

Ein Maler kühlte sein Gelüst—
und malte in der Apsis Grund
den Teufel wüst wie einen Hund.
Da stieß ihn dieser vom Gerüst.

Doch tiefer unten Maria stand.
Die reichte ihm ganz schnell die Hand
und, daß er stehn kunnt, seinem Fuß
den Schnabel ihres winzigen Schuhs—

und sprach zu dem Erschrocknen: ,Sieh,
so lohnt die junge Frau Marie
dem Schelm, der heute schier geprahlt,
doch vordem sie so schön gemalt!'

II. Der Rabbiner

Ein Prager Rabbiner, namens Brod,
gelangte durch teuflische Magie
zu solcher Macht, daß selbst der Tod
vergebens wider ihn Flammen spie.

Doch endlich geriet es dem Tode doch:
Er verbarg sich in einer Rose Grund.
Der Teufel dachte der Rose nicht, und
der Rabbiner starb, als er an ihr roch.

———

Signboards

Our reverence is due those wooden signs
That show a pointing hand and a few lines

Acquainting us with some nearby resort
Or the constabulary's latest thought.

For they embody, where all else is mute,
The voice of Reason, kindly and astute.

Their modest presence here betokens Culture:
Here ruleth Man—no longer bear and vulture.

Die Tafeln

Man soll nichts gegen jene Tafeln sagen,
die eine Hand an ihrer Stirne tragen,

den Namen einer Schenke nahebei,
den Paragraphen einer Polizei.

Sie sind, wenn sonst nichts spricht im weiten Land,
ein wundervoller justiger Verstand.

Bescheiden zeugt ihr Dasein von Kultur:
Hier herrscht der Mensch—und nicht mehr
Bär und Ur.

———

Subdivision

(Recite soulfully)

I am a subdivision
without a house, alas,
an undeveloped vision
all mud and stakes, no grass.

The moon peeks from the clouds—
I beg it: stay inside—
(The moon peeks from the clouds)
My "homes" will be supplied!

I've just received a name.
My name is Withering Height.
My sisters left and right
Were christened much the same.

The agents, Crooke & Gleason,
have pledged their sacred word:
it's signed and sealed, next season
the builders will be heard.

The moon withdraws to heaven
and locks the door behind.
The moon withdraws to heaven—
this is no fault of mine!

Aus der Vorstadt

(Mit Seele vorzutragen)

‚Ich bin eine neue Straße
noch ohne Haus, o Graus.
Ich bin eine neue Straße
und sehe komisch aus.

Der Mond blickt aus den Wolken—
ich sage: Nur gemach—
(der Mond blickt aus den Wolken)
die Häuser kommen noch nach!

Ich heiß auch schon seit gestern,
und zwar Neu-Friedrichskron;
und links und rechts die Schwestern,
die heißen alle schon.

Die Herren Aktionäre,
die haben mir schon vertraut:
Es währt nicht lang, auf Ehre,
so werd ich angebaut.

Der Mond geht in den Himmel,
schließt hinter sich die Tür—
der Mond geht in den Himmel—
ich kann doch nichts dafür!'

———

Scholastic Conundrum I

Just how many angels may
Sit upon a needle's end—
Give due thought to this and say,
Dauntless reader mine and friend!

All! I hear you chortle shortly;
For their girth is not of earth!
And a wraith, however portly,
Needs pure nothing for a berth.

I, however, stake my bit on
None! Remote from human foci,
Surely they can only sit on
Rarefied spiritual loci.

Spitzfindiges

Wieviel Engel sitzen können
Auf der Spitze einer Nadel,
Wolle dem Dein Denken gönnen,
Leser ohne Furcht und Tadel!

Alle! wird's Dein Hirn durchblitzen,
Denn die Engel sind doch Geister,
Und ein wenn auch noch so feister
Geist bedarf schier nichts zum Sitzen!

Ich hingegen stell' den Satz auf:
Keiner! Denn die nie Erspähten
Können einzig nehmen Platz auf
Geistigen Lokalitäten.

———

Scholastic Conundrum II

Can an angel mountain climb?
No. It has too little heft.
Human feet and boots are left
to perform this every time.

If it wants to anyway,
it must reterrestrialize
and assume a maiden's guise:
Miss Amanda Creampuff, say.

One will always notice, mind,
whence she came and what's inside,
for a lady of this kind
has a very special stride.

II

Kann ein Engel Berge steigen?
Nein. Er ist zu leicht dazu.
Menschenfuß und Menschenschuh
bleibt allein dies Können eigen.

Lockt ihn dennoch dieser Sport,
muß er wieder sich ver-erden
und ein Menschenfräulein werden
etwa namens Zuckertort.

Allerdings bemerkt man immer,
was darin steckt und von wo—
denn ein solches Frauenzimmer
schreitet anders als nur so.

———

The Lambkin Cloud

Out of the blue of heaven
A piteous bleat is heard:
A lambkin cloudlet severed
From her ancestral herd.

At Bomst a blimp named *Bertha*
Hears her and climbs in touch,
And guides the dear thing earthward,
Who lost, alas, so much.

Afloat at Bomst's green common,
She hovers in thankful mood;
Three white-clad maids of honor
Proffer her drink and food.

But when the morning had glimmered,
The first new morning at Bomst,
They found she had drifted Schrimm'ard
Whither from Bomst thou com'st.

Die Lämmerwolke

Es blökt eine Lämmerwolke
am blauen Firmament,
sie blökt nach ihrem Volke,
das sich von ihr getrennt.

Zu Bomst das Luftschiff *Gunther*
vernimmt's und fährt empor
und bringt die Gute herunter,
die, ach, so viel verlor.

Bei Bomst wohl auf der Weide,
da schwebt sie nun voll Dank,
drei Jungfraun in weißem Kleide,
die bringen ihr Speis und Trank.

Doch als der Morgen gekommen,
der nächste Morgen bei Blomst,—
da war sie nach Schrimm verschwommen,
wohin du von Bomst aus kommst . . .

———

The Werwolf

A German Werwolf came away
from wife and child one evening, bound
for a dead teacher's burial mound,
and said to him: "Decline me, pray!"

The kindly spirit climbed the boss
on his memorial plaque, and thus
addressed the Werwolf, who had crossed
submissive paws before the ghost:

"Der Werwolf," said the worthy wraith,
"des Weswolfs, genitive, i'faith,
dem Wemwolf, dative it is writ,
den Wenwolf—there's the last of it."

The cases charmed the werwolf's soul;
his chops adrool, his eyes aroll,
he asked the elder: "Won't you add
plural to single number, dad?"

The village teacher, though, confessed
he could not honor this request.
Though wolves were not extinct by far,
"wer" came but in the singular.

The wolf arose with streaming eyes
(his wife and child, you realize!!)
But his was not a scholar's mind:
he parted grateful and resigned.

Der Werwolf

Ein Werwolf eines Nachts entwich
von Weib und Kind und sich begab
an eines Dorfschullehrers Grab
und bat ihn: ,Bitte, beuge mich!'

Der Dorfschulmeister stieg hinauf
auf seines Blechschilds Messingknauf
und sprach zum Wolf, der seine Pfoten
geduldig kreuzte vor dem Toten:

‚Der Werwolf,' sprach der gute Mann,
‚des Weswolfs, Genitiv sodann,
dem Wemwolf, Dativ, wie man's nennt,
den Wenwolf,—damit hat's ein End.'

Dem Werwolf schmeichelten die Fälle,
er rollte seine Augenbälle.
‚Indessen,' bat er, ‚füge doch
zur Einzahl auch die Mehrzahl noch!'

Der Dorfschulmeister aber mußte
gestehn, daß er von ihr nichts wußte.
Zwar Wölfe gäb's in großer Schar,
doch ‚Wer' gäb's nur im Singular.

Der Wolf erhob sich tränenblind—
er hatte ja doch Weib und Kind!!
Doch da er kein Gelehrter eben,
so schied er dankend und ergeben.

Strictly speaking, stanza 3 should read "The whowolf, of whose-
wolf, to whomwolf, (archaic) whonwolf." But since the *wer* syl-
lable has nothing to do with the pronoun "who" but means
'Man,' cognate to Latin *vir*, we shall down arms.

Songs from the Gallows

Galgenlieder

Christian Morgenstern

Translated by Walter Arndt

from "Korf's Drivel-Shrivel"

Korf, who takes himself for model,
Likes his reading swift and spare;
Floods of coarse pretentious twaddle
Daily drive him to despair.
So he builds a tool whereby
The entangled mind is freed:
Scanning-glasses for the eye
Which condense the stuff they read!—
Christian Morgenstern

Christian Morgenstern (1871–1914) was a
German poet, theosophist, and translator whose
nonsense poems have been among the best-
known and best-loved works in Germany
throughout this century. Often compared to the
drolleries of Lewis Carroll and Edward Lear,
Morgenstern's poems are whimsical yet haunt-
ing, a rare blend of humor and odd meta-
physical intimations.

Morgenstern wrote the first of his *Galgenlieder*
after he and some friends had returned from
a carefree outing past Gallows Hill near
Potsdam and formed a "fraternal order of the
gallows." His collection, published in Germany